THE GIFT OF PARENTING

Unwrapping Your Child's Potential

DR. SHANON GIBSON

BALBOA.PRESS

A DIVISION OF HAY HOUSE

Balboa Press books may be ordered through booksellers or by contacting:

Balboa Press
A Division of Hay House
1663 Liberty Drive
Bloomington, IN 47403
www.balboapress.com
844-682-1282

Print information available on the last page.

ISBN: 978-1-9822-6850-3 (sc)
ISBN: 978-1-9822-6852-7 (hc)
ISBN: 978-1-9822-6851-0 (e)

Library of Congress Control Number: 2021909270

Balboa Press rev. date: 05/26/2021

This book is dedicated to my beautiful daughters, Sarah and Michelle. Thank you for choosing me to be your mama. I love you to the moon and back!

CONTENTS

FOREWORD

I am absolutely delighted to write this foreword, not only because Dr. Shanon Gibson has been a friend, colleague, and mentor for nearly twenty years but also because I believe wholeheartedly in the importance of these early connections and setting young children up for success. I also believe deeply that parenting really is the toughest job that most of us will ever do and that it is also one of life's greatest gifts.

There is no such thing as a perfect parent, and even the best moms and dads need information and direction. *The Gift of Parenting* by Dr. Shanon Gibson provides just that. This book covers everything from brain development and behavior to communication and connection and is founded on current research and her personal parenting and educational experiences.

Dr. Shanon Gibson is an expert in early childhood development and education, working with children, parents, faculty, and even state and national officials. I have been blessed to know Dr. Gibson now for many years now, and our connection has developed from supervisor and mentor to colleague and dear friend. I have witnessed her brilliance in action numerous times with her own children, students, teachers, parents, and so many more. When I was a parent to young children, our family grew from a family of four to a family of eight seemingly overnight. We had been foster parents to more than twenty children during the course of five years and, through adoption, became parents of six. Dr. Gibson offered me invaluable advice and support on parenting and coaching children with diverse needs, extensive trauma, and developmental delays. She helped me to manage meltdowns, calm the chaos, and create connections with some kiddos who really, *really* struggled. She *truly* understands what it takes to *unwrap the potential* of young children and is a compassionate guide to those on that path.

Dr. Gibson has helped countless children and families, like mine, over her more than thirty-year career in special education. She understands the behaviors and the needs of young children and is committed to providing them the care and support they need to flourish. In addition to working for the public school system and serving as an advocate and advisor, Dr. Gibson opened her own preschool in order to provide the kinds of foundational lessons she has shared in this book to more children and families in the community and is always reaching out to give someone a hand up. I have listened with admiration as she consults and trains parents, teachers, and therapeutic providers all over the nation. She is also an international educational consultant to the Ministry of Education in Palau, bringing her extensive experience and knowledge all around the globe. She reminds us: "We have to shift out of our cultural focus on teaching cognitive skills in early childhood and move to supporting the development of early social skills, language skills, and problem-solving skills." With her whole-child approach and social/emotional focus, Dr. Gibson offers pearls of wisdom to *unwrapping potential.*

Dr. Gibson recently completed and published an entire curriculum for early childhood educators, soon to be in classrooms nationwide, to provide these social skills lessons and educational enrichment activities to help children "BEE all they can BEE." At every juncture, as in this book, Dr. Gibson reminds us just how imperative these formative years are and coaches us on making the most of this time.

While it is written especially for parents, this book is applicable for a wide range of audiences, from teachers and therapists to caregivers and anyone else vested in the future of humanity. All groups of people have a stake in the success of young children, and the education and care of young children plays a pivotal, often underrecognized role in the connection and direction of our society at large. Dr. Gibson reminds us: "Children should feel valued, loved, and wanted. When we invest in our children, we invest in our future." She begins by explaining why early childhood is *so* important and explains that, "Quality experiences, feeling connected, and feeling safe are so important for young children. We must take the time to invest in children. We must treat children with care and respect." I have found this to be the most indicative factor for success during my experience in the classroom as a behavior specialist and therapist and as a mom and nana. Do they feel seen? Do they feel safe? Do they feel loved? Once we get that covered, we can commence with the ABCs and 123s.

This book provides guidelines to aid in shaping the physical, mental, and emotional development of children. Readers will find aha moments of realization, as well as proven strategies with real-world application for navigating the parenting paradigm. Each chapter is a stand-alone guide to a specific topic, and the table of contents can work like a frequently asked questions guide for parents, teachers, and parenting professionals. Dr. Gibson helps clarify the easily confused concepts of sharing versus turn taking and praise versus encouragement. She helps parents understand the difference between these concepts and when each approach might be more helpful to their children's development.

Throughout her book, you can see her heart for the littles, and Dr. Gibson concludes by providing encouragement and bringing us back to the beginning. Back to the why: It is all about the children and improving the next generation. Children will be richly blessed if their caregivers read *The Gift of Parenting: Unwrapping Your Child's Potential*. I believe that parents and teachers can enrich their connections and strengthen their skills by integrating the concepts and practices presented in this book. This book truly is a *gift*. I am so excited for all of *you* to *unwrap* all this knowledge and wisdom that Dr. Gibson neatly wrapped up and even tied with a bow.

Stacy Rupe, mom and nana
Registered psychotherapist, consultant, coach, educator, and advocate
Colorado Springs, Colorado

INTRODUCTION

The first five years have so much to do
with how the next 80 turn out.

—Bill Gates

So let's start in the best place to start—the beginning. And let's start with
what we know for sure. The beginning is early childhood, and what we
know for sure is that it matters. No, it doesn't just matter. It matters *a
lot*. More times that I care to think, I have heard, "Does early childhood
really matter?" "They are *just kids*. They don't really know anything."
"What happens, or doesn't happen, when a child is two or three or four
doesn't matter. They won't remember it."

These ideas couldn't be further from the truth. Early childhood
experiences not only matter; they are critical in the development of a
whole person, for positive, lifelong outcomes. We know exposure and
experiences, or a lack of exposure and experiences, have a tremendous
impact on later success—not just academic success but social/emotional
success. We spend a great deal of time in early childhood focused on
teaching ABCs and 123s and give little attention to the types of social
skills that will be necessary to be truly successful later in life. We have
to shift out of our cultural focus on teaching cognitive skills in early
childhood and move to supporting the development of early social skills,
language skills, and problem-solving skills. Yes, cognitive development
is important, but we can teach those academic-readiness skills that
are needed while we work to support the development of social skills,

communication, and problem-solving. The truth is that it all matters. If we miss the opportunities in the first five years, we are missing a lot.

Having quality experiences, feeling connected, and feeling safe are so important for young children. We must take the time to invest in children. We must treat children with care and respect. We know these early experiences have a profound effect on lifelong outcomes. Yes, there will be negative experiences for our children. Yes, they will have meltdowns, become angry and frustrated, and be sad. That's all part of the journey. However, the positive experiences should outweigh the negative. There should be more joy and less sadness. Children should feel valued, loved, and wanted. When we invest in our children, we invest in our future. The really cool part is we get to watch our investment grow right before our eyes. We become the witness of our work. Do the work—it will be worth it!

EARLY CHILDHOOD DEVELOPMENT

WHAT DOES IT MEAN?
WHY DOES IT MATTER?

"The best teachers are those who show you where
to look, but don't tell you what to see."

—Alexandra K. Trenfor

L ANGUAGE SKILLS, COGNITIVE SKILLS, SOCIAL/EMOTIONAL regulation, and adaptive and motor development in early childhood all have direct, lifelong effects on children. The work we do in early childhood builds the adult the child will later become. The early years are critically important, and we need to be sure we don't miss opportunities to provide enriching, positive experiences for young children. As a parent, you are your child's first teacher. I know—this is old news. But if we know this to be true, then we must take this responsibility very seriously. We are building brains!

If a child experiences a delay or a disability in any of the areas of development (cognitive, social/personal, motor, adaptive, or communicative), there can be implications later in life. A child who has limited exposure to language-rich opportunities may have academic delays throughout school. A child who is not taught to self-regulate will likely experience behavioral challenges that will make it difficult to make and keep friends, as well as cooperate with their classmates, teachers, and family members. A child who has not had opportunities to develop problem-solving skills and higher-level thinking skills may find some academic tasks challenging.

For these reasons, and many others we will discuss later, it is critical that we do the work—the really hard work—with very young children. We must invest in young children to maximize their success as adults. The investment of our time is the best investment we can make for children. They are counting on us to show up, be there, and lead the way. I get it—it's easy to forget your three-year-old will one day be thirteen and that your thirteen-year-old will one day be thirty. What I know for sure is that it goes by so quickly. One day you are celebrating your child's first birthday, and the next day your child is graduating from high school. You hear it all the time: Don't blink. You will miss it. Don't miss the opportunities to do the good work with young children. There are opportunities every single day to provide enriching experiences that will help prepare them for life. We must give young children the skills they need to become quality, confident, caring, and contributing human beings.

Before we get ahead of ourselves and think we need to run to the nearest teacher store, I am not talking about drill and kill with these skills. I am not talking about ways to make your child smart by focusing on academic readiness. Yes, be sure you are working to develop those cognitive skills. Talk about colors and ABCs and 123s. But don't focus on academic readiness to the exclusion of the other equally important skills. What I am talking about is getting in there, making connections with children, and helping them develop the skills needed to build relationships. Through positive supportive relationships, we can build the necessary social and academic skills children need throughout life.

The first thing we have to do is build a quality relationship with our children. We are nothing without relationships. Relationships are work—real work. They are work to establish, and they are work to maintain. But relationships matter. We must be willing to do the work to develop these positive relationships if we want to ensure children feel safe, valued, and cared for.

Okay, so when did early childhood education become more than just preschool? Do we really need to spend all this time focused on young children and their development? Won't they just figure it out? Will this work? Will what I am doing really make a difference? Honestly, it has always been important. We absolutely need to do the work, and it will matter much more than you can imagine. Let's take a look at the history of early childhood psychology and some of the theorists who had an impact on understanding the importance of childhood development.

In the early years of psychology, early childhood development was disregarded. Frankly, children were not considered by most psychologists to be individuals who could be complex thinkers, solve problems, or make decisions. Those of you who have spent any time with children know this couldn't be further from the truth. Young children are very complex thinkers. They are plotters and planners. If they want that chocolate chip cookie or a toy from the store, they are going to come up with a very complex plan for getting it. And if plan A doesn't work, there is always plan B, which, for most, is a tantrum. What I know for sure is young children can solve problems and make decisions. It is important for us to recognize this and support the development of lifelong skills.

Because most professionals did not believe children were complex thinkers during this time, psychologists and researchers did not feel it was necessary to spend time studying the development of young children. What they knew was that children either developed or didn't. It wasn't really worth giving a lot of thought to the how or why this development occurred. It was believed that the outcome of this type of research would not have any real benefit to society. We now know this was completely off the mark. However, this was the time of the children-should-be-seen-and-not-heard philosophy. The do-as-I-say-not-as-I-do mentality was status quo.

It was not until the early twentieth century that there was a shift in this mentality and in the focus of research. Studies began to be conducted that included children. Many began to show an interest in understanding young children and early childhood development. However, the vast majority of the studies and research being conducted focused primarily on children with abnormalities and/or disabilities. The science wasn't really looking at typical developing children and what we could/should expect. The general purpose of these studies was to help researchers understand early childhood development as it could be related to adult psychology. Truth be told, this research wasn't about the children at all; it was still about the adults. They did not study children for the sake of studying early childhood development. The research focused on the information that could be used to understand adults. The researchers had missed the boat yet again. What we needed were researchers who were willing to focus on true early childhood development.

When it comes to the study of child psychology, John Locke and Jean-Jacques Rousseau are considered trailblazers. Locke is considered the father of learning theory and environmentalism. Scientists like Ivan Pavlov (you know, the guy with the dogs) and B. F. Skinner followed in the footsteps of Locke. Rousseau, on the other hand, focused on developmental psychology and was followed by the likes of Maria Montessori (you know her—there are lots of schools who use her philosophy) and Jean Piaget. The approaches for both Locke and Rousseau were considered a radical departure from earlier ideas about children. These new approaches had an effect not only on the way children were viewed but how they should be educated. These scientists were beginning to look at what we could do to improve and support early childhood development.

Until this time, children had been seen as little adults, and as a result, children were given adult tasks at very young ages. We now know this is completely inappropriate; developmentally, children are not ready for such tasks. The expectation was for children to take on adult work and responsibilities by the age of six or seven. Really? Are you kidding? And then when the children couldn't perform like adults, they were punished, degraded, and disenfranchised. Horrible—just horrible! Whose idea was this? It makes my heart hurt to think there was a time when we really expected children to perform adult tasks with the same accuracy as adults.

For these children, education came in the way of hard knocks and on-the-job training. Their innocence and purity were ignored. When Locke's theory of environmentalism surfaced, a new view of children took hold. Thank goodness! The idea was that children were not little adults. In fact, it was suggested they became good adults because of their upbringing and the quality of their education. What a novel idea. Locke theorized that the child's mind was what he termed a *tabula rasa*. This meant the child's mind was a blank slate—nothing going on in there. He suggested that whatever the mind became was the result of the experiences the child had. He was on to something. I don't know about them being blank slates, but he was on to something nonetheless (Crain 1992).

Yes, experiences matter—both good and bad. However, the mind, or brain, is definitely not a blank slate. There's lots of stuff going on in there. We know this now; we may not have known it then. Children are *not* blank slates. It is crazy how much we have learned about the brain in the last ten years. However, what happens in early childhood, all those experiences, absolutely matter for long-term outcomes—the good, the bad, and the ugly. We definitely need more good than bad!

By the mideighteenth century, Rousseau began exploring the stages of early childhood development: infancy, childhood, and adolescence. Rousseau's exploration of childhood was the first time children had been looked at from a developmental standpoint in psychology. He took the time to really look at what was happening regarding the development of young children. For many psychologists, this was revolutionary. By the late nineteenth century, Charles Darwin began looking at psychological development from his theory of evolution. Darwin believed by studying the development of children, he could describe the evolutionary history of the human species. He wasn't really looking at childhood development to suggest that it, in and of itself, had any real value. Darwin was exploring the topic to support his personal theory. From there, we began to see the work of James Mark Baldwin who studied mental development in infants. His work was most important during this time because it was a major influence in Piaget's theory of cognitive development in children. Piaget's work had a profound effect on the study of early childhood development and continues to do so today.

In the 1920s, Piaget decided he was interested in learning more about children and began to study children while he was working in the Binet Laboratory in Paris. While the work was not as exciting as he had hoped, it did spark his interest in younger children and the way in which they responded to the questions they were asked. He was especially interested in the wrong answers the children gave. He became interested in the child's thinking. He concluded that younger children aren't dumber than adults or older children; they think in a different way. This was really the beginning of the study of what would later become Piaget's cognitive developmental theory. Piaget developed a theory that there were periods of development all children go through. These periods begin at birth and end in adulthood, and there are stages within the periods. He believed the thinking of young children was quite different from that of older children and adults (Crain 1992). His work made it clear we couldn't treat children like little adults because they aren't.

For Piaget, learning didn't come from the teacher; learning came from the child. It is a process that involves discovery and spontaneous invention. Children must be allowed to explore and manipulate their environments as they learn. They have to be offered experiences and opportunities in which to learn. Piaget believed it was important to make learning individual and to gear instruction to the level of the child. He believed a child's interests and style of learning changed over time and was different at different times. Piaget also believed learning should be seen as a process, not a product, and that learning takes place through active discovery, not passive inactivity. He also believed social interactions were critical for learning. He was right! Social interaction is critical for development. It is not possible to begin to see things from another's perspective if you do not engage in social interactions. Bottom line: children need opportunities to have real experiences in real life with real people. This will allow them to figure out things on their own.

BRAIN DEVELOPMENT, RESEARCH, AND EARLY CHILDHOOD

Experts tell us that 90% of all brain development occurs by the age of five. If we don't begin thinking about education in the early years, our children are at risk of falling behind by the time they start Kindergarten.

—Bob Ehrlich

H ONESTLY, I AM NOT EVEN sure where to start with this chapter. There is just *so much* information about the brain and brain development it hard to get a focus. I find the brain fascinating. "This three-pound organ is the seat of intelligence, interpreter of the senses, initiator of body movement, and controller of behavior. Lying in its bony shell and washed by protective fluid, the brain is the source of all the qualities that define our humanity. The brain is the crown jewel of the human body" (National Institutes of Health. 2020).

The brain is really quite amazing. Here's the thing, though—you only get one. Yep, that's it—only one brain per person. To my knowledge, we are not yet doing brain transplants. (Boy, now that's a scary thought.) Because we each only get one, we have to take really good care of them. We have to be sure we feed our brains with good food and good experiences.

The truth is that we are our brains. They control everything we say and do. My daughter once asked me which was more important, the heart or the brain. My reply: "The brain is more important, of course." A person can live with an artificial heart, but there is no artificial brain. Without a brain, a person is considered brain dead. That person is no longer the same. If the brain suffers trauma, it can change the person forever. Trauma to the brain can have an effect on emotions and behavior, just to get started. There is no question for me that the brain is the most important organ in the human body. We must take very good care of our brains. We must work to develop our brains and then keep learning to keep them in shape.

Here's what we know: Neuroscience is exploding. We've learned more about the brain in the past ten years than in the previous one hundred years. Technology has allowed scientists to look inside of our brains and really see how they work. More than 255 brain journals are now being published. Thirty-seven thousand scientists from sixty-two countries produce new study results on the brain daily. We know there are critical windows of opportunity when people learn most and best. These windows of opportunity will come and go and, thus, shut, and we will not have them again. This does not mean there is not an opportunity to learn skills at another time. It just means the ideal time for a particular type of learning no longer exists. We certainly know the brain can be retrained and new learning can occur. The adage that says you can't teach an old dog new tricks is not true. We also know early childhood is a critical time of brain development. We have to be sure we are providing an enriching environment for our children to maximize these windows of opportunity.

Here's what scientists know about the brain development in children (raisesmartkid.com):

- Brain development is a combination of genetics and environment. The genes the child receives from his parents create the structure of the circuit. The combination of nutrition, environment, and stimulation determines how the circuit is wired. Developing the brain is all about the wiring.
- Your child is biologically ready to learn. Remember, a three-year-old's brain is two and a half times more active than an adult's brain. A child's brain has more synapses than an adult's, and the density of the synapses remain high until about age ten.
- Early childhood experiences lead to lifelong outcomes. The quantity, quality, and consistency of stimulation from your child's early experiences contribute to the structure of the brain. Experiences matter.
- It is important to remember there are windows of opportunity in your child's mental development. There are critical periods when your child is ready to absorb specific types of learning.

There are times in development that are called optimal window, next optimal window, and rewiring. These times differ for different skills. Here is a chart to help you better understand these windows:

Window for:	Optimal Window	Next Optimal Window	Rewiring
emotional intelligence	0–24 months	2–5 years	any age

motor development	0–24 months	2–5 years	decreases with age
vison	0–2 years	2–5 years	
early sounds	4–8 months	8 months–5 years	any age
music	0–36 months	3–10 years	any age
thinking skills	0–48 months	4–10 years	any age
second language	5–10 years		any age

www.raisesmartkid.com

That being said, it would only make sense that we would spend as much time as possible developing this amazing and powerful organ. We would certainly understand the importance of brain development in the early years. As a culture, we would value the early experiences from birth to age five and ensure our children received the highest quality environment that supports positive experiences and opportunities for the brain to grow. We would ensure we avoid trauma at all costs, so as not to damage the brain. We would make sure only the best food was eaten so as to properly nourish the growing and developing brain. We would be sure to minimize stress because we know when the brain is stressed, it cannot learn and function properly. We would provide rich, supportive experiences that would support the development of the neural pathways as the brain develops in early childhood. If all of this makes so much sense, why don't we really ever think about it? Why don't we honor the developing brain in early childhood? Supporting brain development in the early years has a direct effect on the brain for the rest of your life.

According to Jack Shonkoff, the director of the Center on the Developing Child at Harvard University, research clearly shows just how important the first few years of life are in terms of overall brain development. The research he and others have done gives us several things to think about.

First, you must understand that at birth we have most of the brain cells we will have for our entire lives; however, there are relatively few of the connections or the circuits between the different cells. This is where the parent and the environment come in. If you are involved with a young child, you are helping to build this brain! Yep, that's right. Brain building is what it's all about. Helping young children make connections is building their brains. Between the ages of three and ten, rapid social/emotional, intellectual, and physical development occurs. Brain activity between the ages of three and ten is more than twice that of adults. Young children are busy—busy growing, busy learning, and busy developing.

According to Shonkoff's research (2012), connections happen very, very quickly. The brain is building synapses. What the heck is a synapse? I am glad you asked. A synapse is a connection that allows for the transmission of nerve impulses. Synapses are found at the points where nerve cells meet other nerve cells and where nerve cells interface with glandular and muscular cells. In every case, this connection allows for the one-way movement of data. The human body contains trillions of these connections, and, at any given time, huge numbers of these connections are active. So the young child is busy making all of the neural connections and we are helping them get the work done. How many connections are they really making? You won't believe it! A baby forms seven hundred new neural connections per second—yep, per second. No wonder they are so busy and tired.

Shonkoff says this is building the architecture of the brain. When you think about it, It's crazy. This child is building a brain they will use for the rest of their life. Will it have a strong foundation? Will it be built on quicksand? Will it be active and alert or slow and sluggish? It all starts here and now. It matters more than most could ever imagine. Shonkoff says the architecture is dramatically influenced by life experiences. While there is a genetic component (they got their looks from their mom, but they get their brain from their dad), the brain is not genetically hardwired. Our environment and experiences shape the architecture of the brain in the first year of life. In the first twelve months, the foundation is being laid.

Second, the brain of a young child is dependent on the responsiveness of the adults they interact with. So, when this adorable baby is doing all the adorable baby things like babbling, cooing, and smiling, the adult response is critical. *Tune in!* Put down your phone, tablet, or other device, and pay attention to your child. It matters.

The way in which the adult responds is helping to shape the circuitry of this growing and developing brain. The research of Shonkoff suggests the back-and-forth responsiveness from the young child to the adult is the critical piece. It truly shapes the brain.

Third, language-rich environments matter. We must talk with young children. We must stop talking *at* them. The research suggests a child with perceived misbehavior hears eighty commands per hour. We do it: Sit down. Stop touching. Be quiet. Come here. Put that away. Stop running. How many times …? Use your napkin. Wash your hands. Oh my. It's just too much for this developing brain to handle. It's just words; it's not language, really.

The developing brain needs a language-rich environment. What does that mean exactly? Shonkoff says we can begin to see the differences in the size of a child's vocabulary as early as eighteen to twenty-four months (2012). He says the differences are not genetically hardwired. Instead, the differences are based on the type of language environment the child grows up in. Dr. Dana Suskind's book, *Thirty Million Words, Building a Child's Brain*, takes a look at language and brain development. Her research, along with that of Betty Hart and Tom Risely, suggests children of professional families are exposed to many more words than those children who are from low-income families. There is a growing concern about the vocabulary gap widening between children from different socioeconomic groups.

Research suggests that by the end of the third year, children growing up in lower-income families may hear up to *thirty million* fewer words than their more privileged counterparts. That's a lot of words, and the impact on early education is tremendous. According to Dr. Anne Fernald, a psychology professor at Stanford University, a five-year-old child of lower socioeconomic status (SES) scores two years behind on standardized language development tests by the time they enter school. In fact, a March 2013 study by Fernald and colleagues, titled "SES Differences in Language Processing Skill and Vocabulary Are Evident at 18 Months," reported that signs of the vocabulary gap are evident before a child is even two years old (Fernald 2013). Research indicates that by age four, children in middle- and upper-class families hear fifteen million more words than children in working-class families, and thirty million more words than children in families on welfare. This disparity in hearing words from parents and caregivers translates directly into a disparity in learning words. This significant lack of language puts a child born with the fewest advantages even further behind.

Of the children born in 2001, only 58 percent of poor children started school ready to learn, as compared to 75 percent of children from middle-income families. The vocabulary gap is supported by the research of Shonkoff. His research suggests a child who grows up in a home with highly educated parents will be talked to more frequently and will be exposed to a more varied vocabulary. Further, a child who grows up in a home with parents who have limited education will likely be spoken to less, will be exposed to a smaller vocabulary, and will not be provided with elaborate descriptions. If early intervention is not provided, it is likely these children will struggle with *language* their whole lives.

This may be a good time to clarify something. The difference between speech and language can be very confusing. So, while we are on the subject and before we move on, let's just take a minute to distinguish between the two. First, speech and language are different. According to the American Speech-Language Hearing Association:

Speech is the verbal means of communicating. Speech consists of the following:

- **Articulation.** How speech sounds are made (e.g., children must learn how to produce the *r* sound in order to say *rabbit* instead of *wabbit*).
- **Voice.** Use of the vocal folds and breathing to produce sound (e.g., the voice can be abused from overuse or misuse and can lead to hoarseness or loss of voice).
- **Fluency.** The rhythm of speech (e.g., hesitations or stuttering can affect fluency).

Versus *language*, which is made up of socially shared rules that include the following:

- What words mean (e.g., *star* can refer to a bright object in the night sky or a celebrity).
- How to make new words (e.g., *friend, friendly, unfriendly*).
- How to put words together (e.g., "Peg walked to the new store," rather than, "Peg walk store new.").
- What word combinations are best in what situations. ("Would you mind moving your foot?" could quickly change to "Get off my foot, please!" if the first request did not produce results.)

OK, I hope that helps. Young children need a language-rich environment. They need to hear words—lots of them. These words help them to prepare for school, social interactions, and life in general.

Next, poverty can have a negative effect on the developing brain. It is true a young child would have no real idea how much or little money their parent(s) have. Certainly, we have all heard stories of adults who did not know they were poor growing up. They had everything they needed, and it was just the way it was. End of story. However, the research would suggest young children can *feel* the poverty. According to Shonkoff's research, the challenges of poverty are not about the level of the family's income as much as it is about how well the parent is able to adjust behavior to create an environment that is safe, secure, and rich with language and experiences for the developing child. If the parent is stressed as a result of the poverty, that parent can disconnect from the child and become less responsive to the needs of the child. At this point, the child is likely to feel the stresses of poverty. According to a study by the Illinois State Board of Education (2001), poverty is the single greatest predictor of academic and social failure in US schools, and this is directly related to early experiences.

Lastly, there are things that can be done to support and encourage brain development at an early age. We have to provide rich learning opportunities for young children. Early intervention works. Many states are addressing this by providing preschool opportunities for all four-year-old children for a reduced cost or for free. These early experiences are valuable for supporting brain development. We must educate ourselves about early brain development and the ways in which adults can provide opportunities. One of the easiest things to do is to talk with your child. A rich language environment with lots of vocabulary is a surefire way to decrease the language gap we see. Take a walk and explore nature. Visit the public library and check out a book. Read to your child. Cook with your child. Engage with your child. It all matters.

Make the most of it.

BOYS AND GIRLS:
DOES GENDER REALLY MATTER?

Men and women are different. I don't think men grow
a brain until 26 or even 30. Girls mature a lot quicker.

—Cyndi Lauper

O THER THAN THE OBVIOUS, ARE there any *real* differences between boys and girls? I mean, kids are kids are kids, right? Right … and wrong. Of course, there are similarities because people are people, and kids are kids. There are developmental milestones that are expected to be reached in all children, so in that regard, there are no *real* differences. However, there are differences between boys and girls, and these differences really do matter when it comes to raising and working with children. Gender is something we should take into consideration; there are real differences in brain development when we are looking at boys and girls. There are some who would suggest these differences are not all genetic and the environment plays a role in some of the noted differences. However, it is important that we take a closer look at the gender differences when it comes to our interactions with young children.

According to Dr. Linda Karges-Bone, the author of *More Than Pink and Blue*, it's not pink and blue but gray that matters. We need to take the time to explore brain development as it relates to gender. The book focuses on the differences between the brains of boys and girls and the ways boys and girls acquire and apply knowledge. Her book looks at the implications of gender in the field of education and, more specifically, the ways to shape classroom instruction. While this may not seem to apply to parenting, it absolutely does.

As a parent, you are providing instruction to your child each and every day. It's just not taking place in a school. Your role is to teach the skills necessary for your child to become a successful, contributing adult. You are your child's first teacher. So, let's take a closer look at some of the research and ideas that can be used to support gender as we teach these valuable life skills to our children.

Because I have been working with children for many, many years, gender has been something I have always taken into consideration. I have two daughters (thankfully); girls are my thing. I get them, and they seem to get me. This doesn't mean I don't like boys. I do, but they are just different. I mean, all kids are different, but boys and girls are really different. I have always said the good Lord knew who to give the boys to, and it wasn't me. Those of you who have one of each—one boy and one girl—have a keen opportunity to see these differences firsthand. As we talk more about these differences, it will be easier for you to see how the differences can have a direct impact on the decisions we make when we interact with our children.

Dr. Karges-Bone shares some gender differences that can be taken into consideration.

- The release of testosterone in gestation may influence boys to have better mathematical and spatial skills and to have a drive toward independent thinking.

While this means that boys tend to be better at math than girls, this certainly does not mean girls are not also good mathematicians. As parents, we have a wonderful opportunity to support the mathematical abilities of our boys, and we need to be sure to provide many opportunities to practice and build these skills with our girls. Dr. Karges-Bone also points out there are studies that show girls who do very well in mathematics frequently come from homes in which there were no sons. In this setting, it is suggested a strong father figure set high expectation for academic performance for the girls. It's interesting to note that I have two high-achieving daughters. Both of my daughters performed well in school, and my younger daughter is an engineer. It fits for us.

- The average boy's brain is 10 percent larger than a girl's brain; however, her corpus callosum is significantly larger. The corpus callosum is the bundle of nerves that connects the brain's left and right hemispheres. This difference in size may explain why girls can complete several tasks at the same time with seemingly little effort.

This would suggest girls are better at multitasking. Duh. We already knew that. Seriously, though, we need to take this into consideration when we are giving tasks to our girls and boys. Boys are going to do better with one task at a time. They will be more likely to complete the task successfully and will be less frustrated with the to-do list. Our girls, by contrast, are likely to take the same to-do list and knock it out quickly, taking on more than one task at a time. Knowing this can reduce our frustration as well.

- More boys than girls have trouble learning to read, and more boys end up in special education classes.

Learning to read is no easy task. Reading is a complicated, multifaceted skill. The only way to get better at reading is to read—a lot—so practice is important. More important is for parents to read to their children every single day. There's a great program out there called 1,000 Books Before Kindergarten. This program helps you track the books you have read with/to your child. Getting one thousand books in before kindergarten is completely doable. I promise. Do it. The idea behind one thousand books before kindergarten is simple.

> The concept is simple; the rewards are priceless. Read a book (any book) to your newborn, infant, and/or toddler. The goal is to have read 1,000 books (yes, you can repeat books) before your precious one starts kindergarten. Does it sound hard? Not really if you think about it. If you read just one book a night, you will have read about 365 books in a year. That is 730 books in two years and 1,095 books in three years. If you consider most children start kindergarten at around five years of age, you have more time than you think (so get started).
> The key is perseverance. Make it exciting. When your child reaches a milestone, give him/her a small reward (stickers, backpacks, books). Most local programs already have a reward system built into place. If a program is not available where you live, join our program today. Most of all be creative!

More information can be found on line at http://1000booksbefore kindergarten.org/1000-books-before-kindergarten-program/. There's even an app for parents to use.

If we know reading is more challenging for our boys, let's do the work to help our boys (and girls) develop those early skills needed to make reading an easier skill to develop.

- Girls develop communication skills earlier than boys, and boys tend to take longer to process a verbal response than girls.

Give them time to process! All of them, but especially boys. What does that mean exactly? It means when you give a command, wait a few seconds to let the child process the verbal information before you give the command again or give a second command. When you repeat yourself without allowing time for the child to process, the child has to start over. Yep. Start all over with the processing. That means you now think the child is just ignoring you and being a complete pain in the ass! Not true (well, not true most of the time; sometimes kids are a complete pain in the ass). When we don't allow for processing time and keep giving the command, our children really have no idea what we are asking them to do. Can you imagine how frustrating that can be? Then, to make matters even worse, we (the grown-ups who are supposed to know what they are doing) become frustrated and aggravated and may even believe the children are defying them on purpose. Trust me when I tell you this is not always the case. Give them a minute to make sense of what you are saying, especially the boys.

While much of what I have mentioned is a generalization, I believe it is important for us to consider gender differences when we are working on becoming awesome parents. As Dr. Karges-Bone says, "Gender, like personality, temperament, learning styles and multiple intelligences, shapes children's reactions to curriculum and instruction." For young children not yet in school, the world and everything in it is the curriculum, and you are providing the instruction. Take the time to teach and use what you know about gender to enhance your instruction.

WHAT IS BEHAVIOR?

If a child doesn't know how to read, we teach.
If a child doesn't know how to swim, we teach.
If a child doesn't know how to multiply, we teach.
If a child doesn't know how to drive, we teach.
If a child doesn't know how to behave, we …
… teach?
… punish?
Why can't we finish the last sentence as
automatically as we do the others?

—Tom Herner

A LL OF US, WHETHER THE child is ours or someone else's, want children to behave. When a child misbehaves, we frequently hold the adult responsible for the child's misbehavior because the adult is supposed to manage the child's behavior or get the child under control. The truth is the adult should *not* be managing the child's behavior. In fact, the job of the adult is to teach—yep, *teach*. Here's the challenge. You can't teach a skill you do not have. It is impossible. So, if the adult can't manage their own behavior, it is unrealistic to expect that adult can teach a child how to manage behavior. So, for the sake of argument, let's assume the adult can manage their own behavior. And let's assume the adult wants to help the child manage their behavior. How do we *teach* a child to behave? Great question, and it's easier said than done. Behavior is hard—I mean *really hard*. Positive behavior is hard to teach. Negative behavior is hard to change, hard to control, and hard to tolerate. Behavior is work. If you want to see real change in negative behavior, you have to be willing to do the work. You must be consistent.

OK, so let's start with what we know. What we know is children are like sponges. They are absorbing information all the time. They are watchers and listeners and learners. So, it only stands to reason they are learning behavior. I firmly believe behavior is learned. If we learn behaviors, then someone or something taught us, intentionally or unintentionally.

One of the leading theories in this field is Albert Bandura's Social Learning Theory.

Bandura (1977) believed children's minds are structured by the environment, the models, and the social training practices the environment provides. Bandura also believed children are more likely to attend to and imitate those people they perceive as similar to themselves. He also suggests children do not learn very much on their own. They are not generally motivated to figure out everything that is out of their grasp. If we want children to learn, we have to be willing to motivate them and then offer assistance with the acquisition of the new skill.

We, as parents and teachers, must teach them new things, be sure we are administering rewards and punishment as needed, and, above all, provide them with appropriate role models so they have the opportunity to see these skills in action. The child will take into consideration what happens to the model when engaged in a particular behavior before the child decides to copy the person's action. For example, if the model is receiving praise from a parent for being helpful, it is likely the child will also attempt to be helpful so they too can receive the attention and praise from the parent. By contrast, if the model is punished for not following the parent's direction, it is likely the child will avoid that behavior so as to avoid disapproval and punishment from the parent.

Another way to think about behavior, or misbehavior, is to think of behavior as a set of skills—social skills, to be more specific. Having good social skills is necessary for a positive, productive, and successful life. Social skills help all of us learn what to say, how to make positive choices, and how to behave in a variety of social situations. We also know having good social skills can influence more than just relationships with friends and family. Positive social skills can impact academic performance as well. The thing to remember is these are a set of skills. And, just like the skills of baseball or soccer, they must be taught.

While most children pick up positive skills as a result of the everyday interactions they have with adults and their peers, it becomes very important that the adults in the children's lives take the time to reinforce these positive skills. We need to be sure children know we are paying attention to the positive skills they are learning. The same can be said for misbehavior or negative social skills. If children are learning behaviors, they can learn negative behaviors just as easily as they learn positive ones. Pay attention to the behavioral models children are exposed to. Most children are going to try out some of the less desirable behaviors to see if they will fly. We have to be ready to replace those negative behaviors with positive ones and be prepared to teach the needed social skills.

So, what are these social skills, and how do we teach them? There are many definitions of social skills, but the best way to think of them is as a set of skills needed to get along with others and to create and maintain satisfying relationships. Social skills are also about being flexible. They are about being able to adjust our behavior to fit a particular situation and our personal needs and desires. Most of us want our children to be good, but what does that really mean? For most, it means listening to others, following directions, being polite, and staying calm. These are just a few of the skills we need to teach our children. They can't just figure this stuff out. So, my suggestion is we come up with a short list of skills we want our children to learn and then take the time to teach and reinforce the skills. My top ten skills are listed below:

1. **Listen to others.** This includes your parents and your peers.
2. **Follow the steps.** List the steps and provide a visual. When you can follow the steps, you are on your way to becoming more independent.
3. **Follow the rules.** The rules matter, and they apply to you.
4. **Ignore distractions.** Tuning out distractions is a big deal. The world is full of things that want to steal your attention. Being able to tune out the distractions will keep you focused on your goal.
5. **Ask for help.** We *all* need help every once in a while. Learn how to ask for help and be gracious about accepting it.
6. **Take turns when you talk.** Turn taking is an important and difficult skill. We have to learn to tune in to others when they are talking and wait our turn to share our thoughts.
7. **Get along with others.** Getting along means you don't always get your way. It means compromise and compassion. It means being a gracious winner and an even more gracious loser.
8. **Stay calm with others.** And stay calm with yourself. Learn to take deep breaths and that everything is not about you. See things from someone else's perspective.
9. **Be responsible for your behavior.** If you did it, own it. Right or wrong, it's yours. Don't blame others for your behavior and your choices.
10. **Do nice things for others.** Have a giving heart. Be helpful to others and make an effort to be kind. Kindness counts.

Let's try to remember something very important: *All* children misbehave. It's their job. They push the limits (some more than others), and they see what they can get away with. It is our job to help guide them in a positive direction. We also have to remember that persistence is a wonderful quality. We want children to persist with a difficult task. We just don't want them to persist after we have given them a very firm *no*! It's a delicate dance between encouraging positive behaviors like persistence and extinguishing the please-please-please behavior. So, what are some common misbehaviors and how can we deal with them?

- **Defiance**
  - Get to the root of his behavior. (What is the function of the behavior?)
  - Set your child up for good behavior.
  - Establish absolute ground rules.
  - Compromise when you can.
- **Tattling**
  - Teach problem-solving.
  - Encourage the development of empathy.
  - Avoid rewarding the child for tattling, as this will only encourage it.
- **Fighting/arguing with a peer or sibling**
  - Teach conflict resolution.
  - Step in.
  - Listen to both sides.
  - Don't allow bullying.
  - Teach children to be friendly. They don't have to be friends.
- **Whining**
  - What is triggering the behavior?
  - Call out whining and make it known it is unacceptable.
  - Don't give in.
  - Be consistent.
  - I use the phrase *try again*. This can serve as a reminder to the child that they will need to adjust the behavior.
- **Talking back**
  - Keep track of when back talk happens.
  - Get calm; stay calm.
  - Don't get into a war of words.

- **Lying**
    - Get to the root of the behavior (function of the behavior).
        o Wishful imaginative play
        o Fear of punishment
        o A desire to brag to friends/classmates to boost status and impress them
        o To avoid something they don't want to do (such as clean up toys)
        o A desire to not disappoint parents when expectations are too high
        o An attempt to get attention
    - Give the child a consequence rather than a punishment.
    - Avoid name-calling. Do not call the child a liar.
    - Be clear about your expectations.

OK, so now let's talk about the real reasons behavior happens. This is what we call the function of the behavior. That's really just the technical term for "Why the hell is this kid acting like a crazy person?"

The function of a behavior refers to the source of environmental reinforcement for it

(Tarbox 2009). The function of behavior is *the reason people behave in a specific manner.* When we say the function of a behavior, we basically mean why the behavior is occurring. While it might be difficult to understand why a person does something (e.g., challenging behaviors such as self-injury or aggression), there will always be an underlying function (O'Neill 1997). People engage in millions of different behaviors each day; however, the reasons for engaging in these behaviors fall into four main categories.

The question we have to take the time to ask is: What is the child gaining by engaging in this behavior? What is the function of the behavior?

- Social attention?
- Escape/avoidance?
- Tangibles/rewards?
- Sensory?

Research has shown function-based interventions are more efficient and effective than interventions that are not matched to the function of behavior.

1. Social attention.

People may engage in a certain behavior to gain some form of social attention or a reaction from other people. For example, children might engage in a behavior to get other people to look at them, laugh at them, play with them, hug them, or scold them.

What can we do?

- Teach how to appropriately ask for/get attention.
- Increase attention for appropriate behaviors. Catch the child being good!
- Offer replacement behaviors.
- Use *start* statements. Avoid *stop* statements.
- Remove the audience.
- Remove the child.
- Use planned ignoring. (This is hard!)
- Reinforce other children for appropriate behavior.

2. Tangibles or activities.

Some behaviors occur so the person can obtain a tangible item or gain access to a desired activity. For example, a child might scream and shout to gain access to a preferred item (tangible item), get a desired food, or access a desired location or event like the playground or computer.

What can we do?

- Teach how to appropriately ask for the item/material.
- Deny access when not appropriately requested.
- Reinforce immediately when appropriately requested.
- Teach waiting! Please teach your child to wait! Practice waiting often.
- Use first/then boards.

- Reinforce approximations. You're not going to get 100 percent, so don't expect it or wait for it. If this is not a skill a child has, they will not be able to give you 100 percent. Be reasonable.
- Use working-for boards.
- Practice delayed gratification in other areas and at other times.

3. Escape or avoid.

Not all behaviors occur so the person can obtain something; many behaviors occur because the person wants to *get away from* something or avoid something altogether. For example, a child might engage in aggressive behavior to avoid an academic task or a household chore. Another child might engage in self-injury to avoid having to go outside to play with classmates.

What can we do?

- Teach how to appropriately ask for help or a break.
- Reinforce and praise compliance.
- Give activity choice. (Allow the child to choose which activity to do first.) Choices are important and help the child to feel in control. Practice making choices, and don't let the child change his mind. Buyer's remorse is important. It will help the child learn the difference between a good choice and a poor choice.
- Wait until the child is ready, but do not allow the child to leave the activity (out wait the child).
- Do not move from the task presented until the request has been met.
- Gain compliance (no matter how small) before moving on.
- Use positive practice (also known as overcorrection).

4. Sensory stimulation.

The function of some behaviors do not rely on anything external to the person and are instead internally pleasing in some way. They are self-stimulating. They function only to give the person some form of internal sensation that is pleasing or to remove an internal sensation that is displeasing (e.g., pain).

For example, a child might rock back and forth because it is enjoyable for him, while another child might crash into furniture or other people. In both cases, these children do not engage in either behavior to obtain any attention or tangible items or to escape any demands placed on them.

What can we do?

- Redirect/interrupt the behavior.
- Increase access to alternative sources of stimulation.
- Give a planned sensory break.
- Bring the child's awareness to the behavior.
- Offer replacement behavior.
- Label the emotional antecedent (excited, angry, frustrated, etc.).
- Work with an occupational therapist and develop a sensory diet.

The most important thing to remember when you are trying to change or shape a child's behavior is it will take time. You have to be patient with the child and with yourself. You also must be consistent. If we want our children to be successful in the world, we have to take the time to teach the socially appropriate skills they will need to move through life. Positive social skills will make all the difference as our children grow.

The old saying "you know how to behave" is tired. Put it to bed! Make no assumptions about a child's understanding of behavior, especially children younger than five. Positive, proactive parenting is the best way to help children develop the prosocial skills they will need. Take the time and make the investment. It will pay off!

Chapter Reminders

- All children misbehave.
- Behavior is learned; therefore, it can be unlearned and replaced.

- Children engage in challenging behavior because it works for them. It serves a function.
- Challenging behavior results in the child gaining access to something (i.e., obtain) or avoiding something (i.e., escape), gaining attention or receiving some kind of sensory input.
- Some challenging behaviors are part of the typical development of communication and self-regulation.
- Self-regulation, or emotional regulation, is developmental and must be taught/learned.
- Chronic, severe, challenging behaviors require systematic intervention to shape, modify and replace.

SELF-EFFICACY VERSUS SELF-ESTEEM

Children cannot be fooled by empty praise and
condescending encouragement. They may have to
accept artificial bolstering of their self-esteem in lieu
of something better, but what I call their accruing ego
identify gains real strength only from wholehearted
and consistent recognition of real accomplishment, that
is, achievement that has meaning in their culture.

—Erik Erikson

THE GIFT OF PARENTING

A CHILD'S SELF-ESTEEM IS IMPORTANT, RIGHT? As a parent, I should work really hard at building my child's self-esteem and be sure no one damages it. A child's self-esteem can be fragile. It is like sacred ground. Don't touch it, be gentle with it, and do not do absolutely anything to diminish that good-old self-esteem. If I want my child to grow up feeling good about himself, then I have to build that self-esteem. It will make my child a better adult. We have been told over and over that self-esteem matters. And it does—to an extent.

Self-esteem is that external voice (the voice of other people that eventually becomes our internal dialogue) that tells us how wonderful we are (or aren't). It is the voice of our friends and family who say things like, "You're so smart," or, "You look so pretty or handsome," or, "Why do you do such dumb stuff?" or, "You look terrible. Go brush your hair." Self-esteem grows or shrinks when we buy into the message we are being sent whether it is true or not. It stands to reason, as friends and family, we would want our children to feel valued and important and powerful. So, we work hard to build self-esteem.

In theory, it's a great idea. If we tell our children how wonderful they are, they will believe it and move out into the world and become amazing. If we tell our children they are not worthy, they will believe that too, and that will damage their self-esteem. This damaged self-esteem will set them up for failure, and they will not be successful. It's a slippery slope to be sure.

It's every parent's dream: a successful, fulfilled, happy child who, ultimately, becomes a capable, balanced adult. There's only one problem. What if they don't (or do) believe what we say? What if they think they are amazing, and others find them annoying and incapable? What if we tell them they are an amazing athlete, but they don't get the college scholarship they were sure was coming their way? Or the opposite could happen too: What if they think they are inferior? What if they don't think they stack up to the expectations of their family, teachers, and peers? What if their peers are unkind and tell them they are bad at sports even though you told them they were great? What if their grades in school don't reflect the strong students you keep telling them they are? This can cause a real problem. Whom should the child believe? Who is telling the truth, and who is just feeding them lines? Being supportive of your child and stringing them along are two different things. It's time to get real. It's time to be honest and find the things that make your child exceptional and powerful!

One of the things that has happened as a result of trying to build up children's self-esteem is we have created a trophy generation. What a disaster! Sorry, but not every child should get a trophy just for showing up. We are not all winners at everything.

The only way a child will figure out they suck at baseball is to let them suck at baseball. Then, and maybe only then, will they quit baseball (after the season is over, please) and move on to find the thing they do best! My girls were good, maybe even really good, cheerleaders. However, neither of them grew up to be a cheerleader. They didn't win every competition, and there were other cheerleaders who were better than they were. That was true then and always will be. So, where am I going with this? Self-esteem is not a bad thing; we need to tell our children they are wonderful and give them positive feedback. But self-esteem is not the only thing.

So, let's talk self-efficacy. You may be thinking, *What the heck is self-efficacy?* Self-efficacy was first introduced by a social learning theorist named Albert Bandura (Crain 1992). Bandura became very interested in social learning theory and has conducted much research on the topic, more specifically in the area of self-efficacy. So, let's define self-efficacy. "Self-efficacy refers to an individual's belief in his or her capacity to execute behaviors necessary to produce specific performance attainments. Self-efficacy reflects confidence in the ability to exert control over one's own motivation, behavior, and social environment" (Bandura 1977, 1986, 1997). Here's the thing: self-efficacy affects all of us and everything we do. We have high self-efficacy in some areas and low self-efficacy in others. If we consistently succeed at a particular task, we will have high self-efficacy in that area. When we believe we are good at a task, we are more likely to continue to work hard on the task, even if it becomes challenging because we believe we are good at it. By contrast, if we believe we are not good at a task, we will probably work with minimal effort and will be more likely to give up when the going gets tough.

OK, so what does this mean for us and our children? How can we build both self-esteem and self-efficacy?

To me, self-esteem should be protected. We do not want people telling our children they are unworthy, unlovable, or incapable. We do need to be sure they have as many joyful and positive experiences as possible. Those negative experiences can certainly have a negative effect on lifelong outcomes, and those negative experiences are going to happen. That's life. It ain't all roses. So, protect your children from bullies, and remember that bullies come in all shapes and sizes. Grown-ups can be bullies too. We know there will be some not-so-great experiences that will challenge self-talk and will require some buildup from us. Be there. Show up. Be honest. Tell your child, "You've got this."

Self-efficacy is really important too. Here's the challenge with self-efficacy: When your child's self-efficacy is significantly higher than their actually ability, it can lead to an overestimation of what they can actually do. This can cause a problem, for example, if they think they are great at snow skiing and take on the expert slope when they should be on the bunny slope; it is not likely to end well. By contrast, if their self-efficacy is significantly lower than their ability, we can see a delay in growth and skill development. The research suggests the best level of self-efficacy is just slightly above actual ability. When this is the case, your child will be more likely to take on and tackle a difficult task and will then gain experience. Sounds like a win-win.

The goal is for children to feel powerful. They need to feel like they have control over their world. Bandura found children with high self-efficacy generally believe they are in control of their own lives and that their actions and decisions have a direct effect on the way their lives are shaped. Wow! Self-efficacy will help your child begin to take some responsibility for the choices and decisions they make—ownership of behavior. This is seriously lacking in many children today. The blame game is real! So, if you help your child feel like they have more power and control, that child will make better choices and decisions? Sounds good to me.

Let's take a look at self-efficacy and motivation. Generally speaking, those with high self-efficacy tend to make more of an effort to complete a task and have developed grit. They will persist until they have mastered or completed the task. The downfall can be when the self-efficacy is higher than the skill level, and the child does not prepare as well as they should have for a task. To me, this is a child who has heard too often that they are more skilled than they really are. You have to monitor your level of praise (self-esteem-boosting comments) and teach humility. A child with low self-efficacy, by contrast, may sometimes show an interest in learning more about an unfamiliar subject area. Encourage this, and be there to be supportive.

Here are a few interesting things about the way self-efficacy can affect a child's thinking:

- If a child has low self-efficacy, they can see a task as being harder than it really is. You may get an attitude that says, "I can't. It's too hard."
- If a child has low self-efficacy, you may see them become unpredictable or inconsistent when they are engaged in a task they don't feel comfortable with.
- A child with high self-efficacy is likely to be a better planner. They will take time to analyze a task before beginning so they can develop the best plan.
- A child with high self-efficacy loves a challenge and obstacles. They are not intimidated by the work. A child with low self-efficacy is more likely to become discouraged and will give up easily.

And this is really interesting:

- A child with high self-efficacy who fails is more likely to blame external factors like not being prepared, not feeling well, or not trying as hard as they could have. A child with low self-efficacy who fails is likely to blame a lack of ability. They think they can't, so they don't.

It only makes sense that a child with high self-efficacy would be a better student. They probably work harder and stick with a difficult task longer.

If you want your child to develop a high level of self-efficacy, you have to teach them a can-do attitude. This means you have to let your child *do.* Allow your child to make choices as early as possible. Offer reasonable, safe choices as frequently as possible. For example, "Would you like the red pj's or the green pj's?" These types of choices give children some power and control in what seems like a powerless world to them. Let your child do things for himself even though it would be easier for you to do it. Encourage persistence by using positive talk like, "You're really trying to make that work," or, "That's hard, and you kept trying." Avoid telling your child they did a great job when you know they did not. Find something else to say instead. "That was a tough game. They were a great team," is better than, "You did a great job. Your team is still the best." They just got beat! How can they be the best? Be honest, be supportive, and give credit where credit is due.

Show up. Be there. Be helpful. Encourage independence. Be a resource for your children, but don't do it for them. Teach them to fish. They will eat forever!

LEARNED HELPLESSNESS VERSUS ACTIVE INVOLVEMENT

Learned helplessness is the giving-up reaction,
the quitting response that follows from the
belief that whatever you do doesn't matter.

—Martin E. P. Seligman

Tell me and I will forget. Show me and I will
remember. Involve me and I will understand.

—Confucius

THE GIFT OF PARENTING

S O, LET'S PIGGYBACK A BIT on the self-efficacy/self-esteem chapter we just finished. When we examine these two topics a bit closer, we find we are working to avoid learned helplessness and to actively involve our children in day-to-day activities so they will have the opportunity to become strong, independent adults. In a nutshell, learned helplessness is a glass-half-empty mindset. Actively involving our children will encourage a glass-half-full attitude.

In the early 1970s, learned helplessness was investigated by Martin Seligman. Like many concepts and theories, the discovery was accidental. Seligman was studying negative reinforcement and dogs. The dogs were placed in boxes, and a shock would come on in the box. The shock could only be stopped if the dogs jumped over a barrier within the box. One group of the experimental dogs, which had been previously exposed to a shock they could not control, did little to work to get over the barrier and stop the shock. Because in the initial experiment the dogs had only discovered a way to turn off the shock either very slowly or not at all, they had determined they had little or no control over the shock, so why bother. Seligman concluded the dogs had learned that nothing they did would affect what was happening to them. So, why do anything? He also concluded this could be generalized to humans, and the symptoms of helplessness in the dogs that were studied were similar to symptoms of depression in humans. The dogs, not unlike children, learned they had limited control over their own destiny, so they became helpless.

The idea behind learned helplessness is that we can be conditioned to believe we have no control over the outcome of a particular situation, even though we absolutely have the power to help ourselves. For this reason, it is critical we empower our children at a very young age. They need lots of encouragement in their lives: "You did it!" "Way to go!" "You've got this!"

OK, so how do we avoid the trap of learned helplessness with our children? What can we do to teach our children to become glass-half-full people? Excellent question. Let's take a look at some of Seligman's work from his book *Learned Optimism* (Seligman 1991) and what we can do to actively engage our children in developing a can-do attitude.

If we go back to social learning theory, we can see how Seligman's ideas about learned optimism become something we truly have control over. The theory suggests one of the ways people learn is through social learning. What this means is that people (children) imitate and duplicate the behaviors of others. In other words, they are watching and doing what they see. For children who are developing their identity and character, we find they are very impressionable to social learning. If their parents or primary caregivers do not have positive, optimistic coping strategies, then it is likely the child will imitate these behaviors and develop a more pessimistic attitude and approach to solving problems (Positive Psychology Program 2017).

So, what does all this mean? Well, if the I-can't pattern of behavior is the model children have, they are likely to develop an attitude of learned helplessness. As parents, it is important we model positive and optimistic ways to cope with challenges and stressors in our everyday lives. If, as a parent, your coping skills are weak, then you will have difficulty teaching positive, proactive coping skills to your children. You must first develop the mindset of a can-do attitude and work to develop strong coping and problem-solving skills. Yes, there will be days when you want to throw in the towel. "I'm done!" or "I can't take it anymore!" are OK ways to feel—just not all day, every day! Remember, problem-solving is directly correlated to intelligence. As adults, we start solving problems (or situations, as I like to refer to them) as soon as our feet hit the floor in the morning. Some of the problems are quick, easy, everyday problems, like what to do for breakfast or which way to drive to work because an accident has been reported. Our ability to solve these quick, easy problems (situations) can determine how the day goes. A positive approach to these situations can mean a positive day and a positive example set for your children.

Generally speaking, there are four basic steps to solving a problem. The first step is to identify the problem. Ask your child: "What's the problem (situation)?" When you identify the problem, I think it is important to determine if this is a big problem or a little problem. You may think very young children will not understand you as you identify the problem and its size, but using the language of problem-solving as early as possible will encourage the language and vocabulary associated with problem-solving.

The second step to solving a problem is to come up with a plan to solve it. Once the problem is identified, you will need to identify the plan. As your children grow and develop language skills, be sure to ask: "Well, what are we going to do to fix this?" Help them brainstorm some possible solutions to the problem. If they have difficulty coming up with possible solutions, give them a little kick start. I recommend you use both examples and nonexamples. For instance, if the problem is your child is hungry, you can give an example of, "Would you like something to eat?" or the nonexample of, "Would you like to take a bath?" This will help add a bit of levity to the situation, show it is not so serious, and demonstrate that there are times when the solutions don't match the problem.

Once we have identified the problem and come up with a plan, it is time to put the plan into action. Carrying out the plan should solve the problem—at least in a perfect world. However, if the plan doesn't solve the problem, then we have the opportunity to try again. This is when the final step gets put into place.

The reflection, or looking back, on the problem and solution will help your child see how this process works and will ensure they feel empowered by following the process. They will have the opportunity to realize they have been actively engaged in the problem-solving process. During this final step, help your child check the results of the original problem. Help your child check to see if the plan they developed solved the problem. If it did not, then were they able to try again? If they did try again, did it solve the problem? Help your child analyze the outcome of the plan to determine if there was a win-win solution.

Having a plan is a surefire way to get a problem solved. Teaching your child to plan and execute the plan is a life skill. Actively engaging your child in the problem-solving steps will ensure that child sees the power they have to make necessary changes.

TEACHING WAITING
AND BOUNDARIES

All things come to those who wait.

—Violet Fane

Patience is a key element to success.

—Bill Gates

Patience is the ability to put our desires on hold for
a time. Patience is a rare and precious virtue.

—Dieter F. Uchtdorf

O NE OF THE MOST DIFFICULT things to do is to wait for something you really, really want. The ability to wait is often associated with maturity. The older you get, the easier it is to wait. Right? The assumption is adults should know how to wait and should have a good understanding of boundaries and personal space. This could not be further from the truth. Have you been to Walmart? Many adults can't wait, and they sure as hell don't understand boundaries *or* personal space. For goodness sake, move your damn cart out of the middle of the isle and wait your turn! In fact, I know plenty of so-called mature adults who can't or don't wait well. These are the people who drive right on your tail and honk the very second the light turns green. What the hell? Take a breath, and hold your horses. The truth is some adults have such a difficult time waiting that their impulsivity has landed them in jail. If these adults can't wait and don't understand boundaries, how in the world will they be able to teach their children?

Excellent question! I speak for myself when I tell you that I use the skill of waiting *every single day* as an adult. When I say skill, I mean *skill*. Waiting must be taught, practiced, developed, and refined. It is a skill to be taught and learned. I can only hope the teacher is good at waiting so the child has the opportunity to see what good waiting looks like. I feel confident all of you have seen *Willy Wonka and the Chocolate Factory*. Remember Veruca Salt? Yep. She wanted it *now*, and she went down the shoot with the bad eggs. We definitely don't want children who are demanding, impulsive, and aggressive because they lack the ability to wait. We don't want a bad egg—ever.

Another challenge for many of our children is understanding boundaries. By boundaries I mean physical and personal boundaries. Children need to learn to respect the personal space of others. They need to learn what belongs to them and what belongs to others. Nope. Not yours. Don't touch. That's mine, and I am not willing to share. We don't want children who are space invaders and lack an understanding of personal space and boundaries.

Understanding both waiting and boundaries are life skills. As adults, we are presented with opportunities to wait on a daily basis. We wait at traffic lights, in grocery lines, for our oil to be changed, for our turn to use a public restroom, and for our favorite television show to begin. Heck, we even have to wait for instant oatmeal and instant coffee. What the ...? Waiting is a part of life, and the better you are at waiting (the more patient you are), the easier and more joyful your life can be. Obviously, there are some things that require more patience than others, and there are times and events that test our patience. The waiting just always seems to be there, every damn day!

As adults, it also necessary to understand personal and physical boundaries. We can't just take what we want when we want it. We can't take things that don't belong to us. We go to jail for that! We must also respect the personal space of others. If someone invades our personal space, we can feel very uncomfortable. Have you ridden on the subway in New York at five o'clock on a Friday afternoon? Talk about invasion of personal space. If this is not something you are accustomed to, it can make you feel very uncomfortable. It can make you claustrophobic even if you are not typically bothered by crowds. Teaching our children about personal bubbles, or personal space, is important. We don't like it when others invade our space, and we must learn to respect the physical boundaries of others.

As I said, understanding boundaries and learning to wait are necessary life skills. Because these are skills, they *must* be taught. So, the question is, who is teaching these skills? Many of us teach these skills incidentally. By this, I mean that as parents and teachers, we naturally provide opportunities for our children to practice waiting. We use the word *wait* in context, and our children begin to understand what it means. When our children are very young, we expect them to wait, sometimes for extended periods of time, and children doesn't really understand the concept of waiting. Sometimes as adults we become frustrated when our children become agitated and emotional when we ask them to wait. I ask you to step back and take a look at what you are asking young children to do. Is what you're asking reasonable? Are they capable of waiting? How long should they wait? Often, our children lack the skills to wait.

So, what's involved in the skill of waiting? Waiting is not really any different than teaching any other skill. Just like reading or math, you must start where your child is. By this, I mean that if the child can't successfully wait for fifteen seconds, they can't wait for one minute.

That is an unreasonable expectation that will frustrate both you and your child. Breaking down the skill of waiting is an excellent place to start. We need to take the time to build this skill. We need to teach and allow for practice to build the skill.

Here are a few examples to try. With your toddler, when you are preparing to take a bath, fill the tub with water and then say, "Look, the tub is ready for you. Let's wait." Then count one, two, three, and say, "Look, you waited! Nice waiting." This will put the word *waiting* in context, and the child will begin to gain an understanding of the concept. Begin to notice when you are waiting, and if your child is with you, point it out. Notice when you are waiting at a traffic light, the deli counter, or the doctor's office. Say, "We are waiting for our turn. It's hard to wait, but we are good at it." Perfect practice makes perfect.

Our hope and expectation is our children will learn to wait patiently without pouting or stomping their feet in protest. Some of our children become skilled at waiting and are naturally patient. Others, however, don't wait well at all. They are the Veruca Salts of the world. They want it now, and they mean *now*. Teaching the skill of waiting is something that needs to be more deliberate with our children. We cannot assume they will figure it out. When our children don't wait well, we become frustrated and angry, and our children test our patience. You want your child to be good at waiting. You want your child to wait patiently. Find opportunities to feed your child with positive praise when they are waiting. See it, praise it, and teach it.

Now that your child is developing the skills to wait, we will shift to teaching boundaries. It is important to remember a young child has difficulty understanding personal space and physical boundaries. These are also skills we need to build. We also build these skills through practice, so we need to create opportunities to remind children about boundaries and the personal space of others. When my girls were preschoolers, we were involved in a preschool co-op. Our co-op had about thirty-five families. It was a wonderful, positive experience and provided my children with lots of social learning opportunities.

One morning one of the little girls came to school covered in the remnants of her mother's failed attempt at makeup removal. This little girl had helped herself to her mother's makeup drawer. Her lips were a lovely shade of pink, and her eyebrows were massive. Her cheeks were rosy, and her eye shadow was on point. Mom was clearly frustrated, but this was one very proud child. We all got quite a chuckle as the child pranced into school that morning looking like a hot-mess express. Mom shared that this was something that happened far too frequently, and she had not a clue what to do. While I am by no means the perfect mom, I can assure you my daughters *never*—and I mean *never*—went into my makeup bag or drawer. Not *ever*. That is mine, not yours; don't touch it without my permission. *Period*. If you choose to do so, there will be a consequence. It was a clear line in the sand—a boundary. There was not question. We didn't use my makeup to play dress-up because I did not want to confuse them. It was mine and not a toy. I often see moms who allow their children to play and unpack their purses. Your purse is not a toy for your child's entertainment. Don't be surprised when your child begins to dig in someone else's purse or wants to play in your purse at a most inopportune time. As soon as you say the dreaded *no*, get ready for the shit fit.

These are just a couple of examples, but it happens so often because those boundaries are not clearly drawn. When your children have free range at home, they are pretty sure the world belongs to them. It does *not*, and they will be checked at school. Teachers don't do: "Help yourself because you are in charge." In fact, they do: "No thank you. That is not yours, and you are in my space." The my-way-is-the-only-way attitude can make for a very difficult year of kindergarten. Please, please set those boundaries early, and by early I mean as soon as your child can reach for things and certainly as soon as they are on the move. Your child is *not* in charge. Don't give up your control and authority. Set the boundaries.

INDEPENDENCE VERSUS
SELF-DIRECTED BEHAVIOR

Don't handicap your children by making their lives easy.

—Robert A. Heilein

It is easier to build strong children
than to repair broken men.

—Frederick Douglas

RAISING CHILDREN IS NO JOKE! It's work—real work. So, how do you know if you're doing it right? Well, honestly, I'm not sure you do. Half of the time you go with your gut, and the other half of the time you feel like you've been kicked in the gut. Next thing you know, you've become your mother—or your father—and you're doing all the things your parents did that you swore you'd never do if you ever had kids. There is likely one thing you know for sure: You know you want to do your best to raise this kid so they won't live with you forever. Yes, you'll be sad when your child is grown up and ready to leave the nest (not really—promise). And yes, you'll be proud of who your child has become (and may even give yourself a pat on the back). But it will be no easy task to create this independent, contributing member of society. There are many paths your child can take, and some of them are not so pretty. Some are bumpy and rough, and others are filled with sunshine and buttercups. It is the parent's challenge to find the balance as you raise the child the universe has entrusted to your care. This chapter will focus on the difference between independence and self-directed behavior. There is a difference—at least there is for me—and I want to share my perspective on the topic.

When my girls were born, I knew I wanted to raise strong, independent women. My goal was to teach them to rely on themselves. I wanted them to want a partner, not *need* a partner. I wanted them to have a voice—a loud voice—if they felt the need to use it. I wanted them to do whatever they wanted to do (within reason, of course). I wanted my daughters to know no boundaries and to reach for their goals. It goes without saying this was *not* the way I was raised. I had to fight to become independent and freethinking. I don't recall people ever telling me I could do anything I wanted and that they had my back. Nope, never happened for me. So, I was going to make damn sure it happened for my daughters. I had a goal. I just needed a plan. The one thing I knew for sure was the difference between a goal and a dream was a plan. I needed a plan. My goal was strong, independent daughters; my plan was anything opposite of what my parents had done.

I feel confident most of you reading this book are not unlike me. You also want to raise strong, independent children. You want them to be good citizens. You want them to be financially independent and move out of your house. All of these are excellent goals. So, what's your plan? Do you have a plan, or are you just winging it, praying you're able to keep it out of the ditch? Newsflash. That is not a plan! You can do better. If you're reading this book and your child is eight or nine or ten, and you feel like you're already in the ditch or you're headed that way, don't lose hope. You can recover; it's just going to take work. If you're reading this book and your child is younger than three, *yay*! You are in the prime years to create that strong, independent child. Let's get to work!

Let's start with the difference between independence and self-directed behavior. For many, independence and self-direction are often seen as similar and positive behaviors. I suppose having a child who was engaged in self-directed learning could be a very good thing. This would mean the child had initiative and was a self-starter. It could mean they are independent. For me, however, I see these terms as very different. Allow me to explain my perspective.

Children who are self-directed in their behavior move through the world as if they own it—all of it. They are the my-way-or-the-highway kind of kids. They believe their wants, needs, and desires are all that matter. These children frequently lack compassion and an understanding for others' feelings or needs. They take what they want, when they want it. They have few, if any, limits or boundaries, and they are not interested in anyone setting any limits or imposing boundaries. If anything or anyone stands in the way of getting what they want, a temper tantrum is likely to follow. And I do mean temper tantrum, not a meltdown. (I'll talk about the difference between the two of these in a later chapter.) If you think this sounds like a typically developing two-year-old, you'd be right. But what if this is a four-year-old or, better yet, a fourteen-year-old? Then this child would be a brat or just a pain in the ass.

I can tell you I know adults who throw a temper tantrum when they don't get their way or when the universe sets some limits. These people have grown up with a self-directed attitude. I cannot tell you the number of times I have had parents tell me their child is *so* independent. "She's only three and just so independent. She won't let anyone help her. She just wants to do everything for herself." Everything? Really? She's three! The answer is a hard *no*. A three-year-old can't do everything for herself.

"He's so independent! He can get the kitchen chair and push it across the room to the counter. He can climb on the chair and then the counter and get the Cheez-Its from the shelf in the cupboard." The Cheez-Its are on the shelf in the cupboard for a reason. They are not open season. Listen, I am all for encouraging children to do for themselves—that is independence. But limits must be set. So, what does this really mean?

For me, self-directed behavior occurs when the child attempts to develop autonomy (independence) and pushes past the limits that have been set by a parent or teacher. This is a child who has decided to test the limits and see if you are serious about the line in the sand. This child is thinking, "Bet they don't mean it. Bet they won't follow through." It's a test, folks. You better pass, or you're going to get more of the same. Does no mean no?

Pushing past the limits and testing boundaries is typical behavior. Don't be surprised when it happens, but you need to be prepared. These children can be incredibly persistent and are often very bright and inquisitive. The challenge is they can also be very manipulative. They will push until they win. Allowing a child to be self-directed is the path of least resistance. It is certainly easier to say, "What did I tell you about climbing on the chair to get the Cheez-Its?" and then pouring them a bowl full and saying, "I don't want you to do that again, you hear me?" You have just allowed the behavior and reinforced it by giving the child the snack and a free opportunity to break the rules. You may say, "Well, it's not really a rule." OK, then it's allowed, permitted, and encouraged.

Be clear in your rules so you are ready to enforce them. You can't have it both ways. If you allow your child to push past the limits and boundaries and grab a snack off the top shelf, then don't be surprised when, at sixteen, that child pushes past you and grabs the car keys for a quick trip to see a friend, even when you have said no. The response will be, "What are you going to do about it?" That's my question too. Small children equal small problems. Big children equal big problems. Your three-year-old will be thirteen. If it's not cute at three, I assure you it will not be cute at thirteen.

Independence is the goal, and for me, it is very different from self-directed. A child who is independent is curious, inquisitive, interested, and engaged. These children are thinkers and problem solvers. They want to do things for themselves and will become upset and frustrated when you take over and do it for them. Encourage these independent behaviors; in fact, you should teach and foster these behaviors. Offer help only when needed and adopt the try-it-yourself-first approach.

Children who are more self-directed tend to cross the invisible don't-you-dare parent line far too frequently, and it is exhausting! These children are difficult to redirect, and their behavior escalates when they are stopped. They are also masters of engaging in less desirable behaviors at the most inappropriate times (generally in a public place surrounded by thousands of people). They do this for a reason. They know exactly how to embarrass you and that you will likely give in and allow this otherwise unacceptable behavior. They win. You lose.

Think of it like this: You are taking a walk through the neighborhood with your sweet little two-year-old. She starts off in the stroller, and all is well. Then she decides she would like to walk. Not a problem. She's done this before and is very compliant. So, you take her out of the stroller, and she begins walking with you. Suddenly, something catches her eye. She's curious, and I love curiosity. However, the thing that caught her eye is on your neighbor's front porch. She heads for the driveway and is making a beeline for the porch. Do you let her go? Is it OK to run up to the neighbor's porch? Can you just go on another's property without permission? For me, the answer to all of the above questions is *no*. No, she can't go because she has no real reason to be on their property. She is not invited, she is not a visitor, and it is not her house (boundaries, people). If you let her go, she will likely assume it is OK to repeat this behavior on future walks. Do you want to chase her in and out of your neighbors' driveways as a matter of routine? You want her to understand that this space is not hers and that she can't go on another person's property without reason or permission. I would not want a random person entering my property without permission.

She is exhibiting self-directed behavior. She is on a mission—a personal mission—and it is your job to stop her. It is your job to set the boundaries and limits. You will likely meet with some screaming and kicking, as you have interrupted her mission. Hold your explanation for your intervention until she has calmed down. Tell her this is not her house, and she doesn't have permission to be there. Take her back to the sidewalk or street and continue your walk. Block and redirect each attempt to return to the driveway until you have won the battle. If you don't, be prepared for your child to feel free to enter your neighbors' property at her own whim.

Supporting curious, independent children is the goal. Providing limits for self-directed behaviors will help children learn to work with boundaries and will encourage more independent behaviors. It is important to take the time to examine your children's behaviors to determine if they are exhibiting independent behaviors or whether the behaviors are more self-directed. Be honest with yourself. If you see self-directed, you may need to get busy setting limits and establishing boundaries.

HOW TO BUILD RESILIENCE IN CHILDREN: BE A RESOURCE NOT A WHITE HORSE

I learned that courage was not the absence of fear,
but the triumph over it. The brave man is not he who
does not feel afraid, but he who conquers that fear.

—Nelson Mandela

I am not afraid of storms, for I am
learning how to sail my ship.

—Louisa May Alcott

S O, WHAT IS RESILIENCE? WHAT does it actually mean when we say someone has overcome so much and they are resilient? According to Karen Young (2018), "Resilience is being able to bounce back from stress, challenges, tragedy, trauma or adversity. When children are resilient, they are braver, more curious, more adaptable and more able to extend their reach in the world." This is it! This is exactly what I want—a child who is resilient. I want to raise a child who is brave and adaptable and curious and has a positive effect on the world. This, my friend, sounds like one amazing human being. This is a citizen of the world who can't be stopped or knocked down. The question is, how do I raise such an amazing person? What should I, as this tiny human's parent, be doing to build a resilient child? Let's talk about what this means and how we, as parents, can work to build resilience in our children.

The first thing to remember about resilience is it is not something children have or don't have. Resilience is a skill that develops as your child grows (www.psycom.net). Because it is a skill, it can be taught and developed, just like any other skill you are teaching your child. As parents, we can be there to encourage and support our children as they learn to trust their instincts and move out of their comfort zones. We can be there to help our children become problem solvers. We can be there to encourage and support when they are learning a new skill and just need to know someone is standing by to catch them if they stumble.

So, let's take a closer look at resilience and how we, as parents, can help build this much-needed skill. Resilient children (people, for that matter) have internalized the message that they are strong and capable. They believe they are capable of confronting and working though their challenges (www.psycom.net). One of the best ways to build resilience in young children is to allow and encourage them to solve problems independently. You may be saying to yourself, "For goodness' sake, how many problems can a four-year-old have?" Trust me. Four-year-olds have lots of problems. For example, they have difficulty pulling up their pants after using the bathroom or putting on their socks without getting them twisted or putting their shoes on the correct feet. (I have never understood how they can't know their shoes are on the wrong feet.) Their challenges look different from yours; however, these challenges are no less daunting than yours. If we can help our children work through these challenges, they will come out the other side feeling confident and powerful, one challenge at a time.

Another way to build resilience is to provide your child with opportunities to take healthy risks. To be honest, we have made a young child's environment so safe (too safe in many ways). We have eliminated swings and merry-go-rounds from playgrounds, playgrounds are padded with rubber so our children can't get hurt, and helicopter parents are low flying these days. Don't get me wrong. I don't want to see any child injured, but I think we sometimes take it a bit too far. I can't tell you the number of swings I stood up in or jumped out of. How many of you stood on your bicycle seat as you rode down a hill—without a helmet, no less? Clearly, that was not the best idea; however, I am still here. My point is this: pushing your children out of their comfort zones while providing the necessary level of support will help them to learn they can do it, whatever *it* is. This will help them to learn to challenge themselves.

So, what does this look like in young children? It looks like you, the parent, trusting your children and giving them some space to explore their environment. It looks like allowing them to pick up that pebble and explore it but being there to stop them from putting it in their mouths. Be a boundary but not the stop sign. Be sure they are safe but allow them to explore and test the limits. Be mindful without hovering. A little dirt won't hurt. It washes.

One of the most important things we can do is teach our children to be problem solvers—to be thinkers. This seems like it would be an easy thing to do, but it doesn't come as naturally as one might think. It is much easier, and faster, for parents to solve problems and fix things for their children. This, however, is not helpful in the long run. My motto is: Be a resource, not a white horse. Stop riding in to save the day. Your child, generally, *does not* need to be saved. They need to be taught— taught to see the problem, think about the possible solutions, and solve the problem. I know what you're thinking. How does this apply to an eighteen-month-old? It does, trust me.

Very young children are exploring and learning at an amazing rate. They are relying on us, the adults, to be there to provide them with direction and support. Even before children are able to communicate verbally, they are assessing their environments, working through problems, and coming up with solutions. When you see your nine-month-old crawling toward the steps, you have several options. You can run quickly and scoop them up and turn them around, saying, "Danger. We don't go near the steps." You can immediately put up the baby gate so the child is unable to get to the steps and will lose interest. Or, you can move in for a closer look and then let the child size up the situation and go for it. Let them attempt to crawl down the steps or show them how to position their body to do it safely. Let them practice a time or two. Be there, show up, and let them solve the challenge. They can do it with your help.

So, here are some strategies to help build resilience in your child (Hurley 2018).

First, it is recommended you build a strong emotional connection with your child. What we know is children build strong coping skills within caring relationships. This means spending one-on-one time with your child will strengthen your relationship with your child. It also means you need to put down your phone and be present with your child. Positive adult relationships help a child feel safe and engage in experiences that will help them develop positive problem-solving skills.

As parents, another way we can build resilience in our children is to promote healthy risk-taking. By this, I mean we are pushing our children out of their comfort zones a bit. It means encouraging them to do something that might seem a bit uncomfortable to them. This usually looks like trying a new sport or trying out for a part in the school play. It could be talking to the new kid at school who seems a bit shy. Healthy risk-taking means failure is minimized if the child is unsuccessful. No one gets hurt, and there is likely some growth for the child. It means that you, as the parent, are there to provide ongoing support to the child as they move through the new activity. Hurley says, "When kids avoid risk, they internalize the message that they aren't strong enough to handle challenges. When kids embrace risks, they learn to push themselves." Ultimately, we want our kids to know that they've got this!

It is so easy for us, as parents, to want to fix the challenges our children face. Here's another way: When your child comes to you for help with a problem or situation, resist the urge to jump in and take over. I recommend this even with very young children. You want to be the guide in these situations. Rather than telling the child how they should fix the situation, begin to ask questions about the situation. By asking questions, you will guide your child to the solutions and will help them learn to be better thinkers.

Be sure you are labeling emotions and demonstrating coping skills. Most children only recognize three basic emotions: mad, happy, and sad. We want to build that emotional vocabulary every chance we get. We want to label in the moment and notice what the child's body is doing. This will help the child internalize the emotion and better understand what is happening. Dr. Becky Bailey, developer of Conscious Discipline, recommends the use of what she calls feeling buddies. The feeling buddies help children see their emotions and build that emotional vocabulary. It is important to remember mad and frustrated are not the same. Dr. Bailey calls them cousins. This is also the case with sad and disappointed. Again, they are not the same emotion, more like cousins. Teaching both in context is important. It is also important to remember it is not the emotion that gets us into trouble; it is our reaction to the emotion that gets us into trouble. This is where the coping skills come into play. Being angry is OK; throwing things and hitting people is not OK. We much teach our children to manage their emotions. Understanding and managing emotions will build resilience in your children.

We have all made mistakes. Mistakes help us grow. If we want to raise resilient children, we need to help them embrace their mistakes. Hurley says, "Failure avoiders lack resilience. In fact, failure avoiders tend to be highly anxious kids. When parents focus on end result, kids get caught up in the pass/fail cycle. They either succeed or they don't. This causes risk avoidance."

We need to embrace mistakes to help our children see a growth mindset. We need to teach our children that mistakes help us learn. Little kids equal little mistakes. Big kids equal big mistakes. I would much rather my children make mistakes when they are little (little mistakes) and learn from them than rescue them when they are big and making big mistakes.

When my children were little and wanted to buy a piece-of-crap toy at the dollar store, I adequately warned that it was a poor investment and would likely break before we got home. If they insisted, I would allow the purchase. More times than not, the toy was broken before we got home (like I said, but nobody listens to me). My disappointed children had made a small mistake in making this purchase. Now was my time to talk—not lecture, just talk about it. I would also be prepared to remind the next time. These little mistakes add up and help children develop a sense of understanding about making mistakes and learning from them. Mistakes can be good for growth. Be there to help your children see the value in the mistakes.

Can you believe optimism and resiliency go hand in hand? Who would have guessed? Glass half full equals resilient attitude. As parents, we have the opportunity to nurture optimism in our children. If your children tend to be more glass half empty, acknowledge their feelings and help them work to reframe their outlook and teach them to see things in a more positive light.

Last but not least, go outside. Put down the tablet, turn off the television, and take your children outside. It has been shown that exercise helps to strengthen the brain and make it more resilient to stress and adversity. Sports activities are great, but children also just need time outside to play, ride their bikes, kick a ball, or climb a tree. Find an outdoor activity your children enjoy and encourage them to get outside.

Helping children know things are not always perfect and things are bound to happen that we didn't expect will support them as they develop resiliency. We need to let our children know they are loved unconditionally. This will give them a solid foundation to come back to when the world begins to feel a bit overwhelming or unsteady. Eventually, your children will learn they can build a solid foundation for themselves. A big part of resilience is building a solid belief in themselves as thinkers and problem solvers. Believing in themselves is the best thing they can ever believe in!

THE IMPORTANCE OF FLEXIBLE THINKING

It does not matter how slowly you go
so long as you do not stop.

—Confucius

I'M STUCK. NOT PHYSICALLY STUCK but mentally stuck. I know what I know and believe what I believe. You can't change the routine—ever. I need sameness and consistency. I don't like change. I need to know what's coming next. I need it to all make sense and be predictable. Don't move my cheese; I can't handle it—ever! Signed, your child.

OK, OK, I get it. For some of us, change is difficult. We like the sameness and familiarity of the things that bring us comfort and make us feel safe. Change can make us feel scared. Not knowing what is coming next or what to expect in a given situation can be unnerving. Change can cause stress and anxiety. Truth is, if change is difficult for us as adults, with all our logic and coping skills, can you imagine how difficult it can be for your child?

Change is inevitable. Change is the only thing we know for sure. Change is easier to accept if we are flexible in our thinking. When unexpected changes occur or things don't go our way, our thinking and problem-solving get thrown off. We short-circuit and get stuck. It is difficult to move forward because our thinking is rigid. Rigid thinking increases frustration and anxiety. Rigid thinking means your child has difficulty switching gears when things change, even if you have tried to explain the change. This can cause tears, aggression, yelling, and feet stomping or just a plain old, drop-to-the-ground meltdown. It can cause our children to miss out on enjoyable activities because they wanted to do one thing and not another. Perhaps your child wanted to go swimming, but it started to rain so you decided to go see a movie instead. If your child thought they were going swimming, they may have difficulty making the shift and may become very upset about not getting to swim. This may cause them to miss out on the movie too, all because they couldn't be flexible in his thinking. Having a child who is a rigid thinker or who lacks flexibility in their thinking, often means parents do everything they possibly can to *avoid* a change in routine, schedule, location, menu, and so on. By avoiding the dreaded change, you can avoid the damn meltdown. Thank God we can avoid the meltdown. The meltdown is downright embarrassing, especially if the grocery store has run out of the favorite chocolate chip cookie and only has the unacceptable sprinkle kind. You may think, *Good Lord, help me! I am doomed because my child is a rigid thinker and is absolutely* not *flexible—at all.*

Maybe it's not as bad as you think. I mean, after all, he is only four. How flexible can a four-year-old be anyway? It's just easier to follow his lead and avoid the meltdown at all cost. That's the best plan, right? *No.* It's not the best plan and not helpful to your child in the long run. We *must* teach flexible thinking. We must practice flexible thinking.

According to Katie Hurley, licensed clinical social worker, "Cognitive flexibility includes two skills: flexible thinking and set shifting. Kids who are able to think about a problem in a new way engage in flexible thinking, while kids who get stuck in their ways tend to engage in rigid thinking. Set shifting refers to the child's ability to let go of an old way of doing something to try a new way" (Hurley 2020). Kids who get stuck will inevitably miss out because they can't move on. For example, if you meet some friends at the park and your child says, "I can't wait to swing," you know he will be disappointed if the swing is being used, out of order, or just plain not there. As a parent, you may try to prepare your child for the possibility the swing won't be available. You may even present a few hypothetical situations, some what-ifs in hopes you can adequately prepare your child for what might be coming. You arrive at the park only to find your predictions were correct. The swings are full of happy children who don't look the least bit interested in leaving their current swinging madness. Now your child has to wait and annoy you with the ever constant, "When will it be *my* turn," or, "I've been waiting *forever.*"

You say, "How about the slide?" Or, "Let's try the monkey bars." But much to your dismay, he ain't budgin'. You tell him you only have a few minutes to play, but that doesn't matter either. So, the lack of flexibility means there is a strong likelihood your child will miss out on all his playtime at the park. He wanted the swing, only the swing, and is not changing his mind under any circumstances, so we will wait ... and whine.

At the end of your visit to the park, your rigid-thinking child is not ready to leave because he has *not* had his turn on the swing, and that means he has not had an opportunity to play. His lack of opportunity to play is a direct result of his unwillingness to engage in *any* other activities on the playground. He had lots of opportunities and chose not to act upon them, which is not your fault. But holy crap, what are you thinking asking him to leave before he has had time to play? Are you crazy? You prepare yourself for the inevitable, impending, full-on meltdown. You know it's coming. He didn't get to swing, which means he didn't get to play, which means there will be a full-on meltdown when you ask him to leave. Damn. A scene at the playground again!

You get the picture. And the truth is, at some point, we go down this road with (almost) all children. It is part of the developmental process. The ability to be flexible takes practice and patience. So, let's help our kids become more flexible in their thinking by helping them practice.

When kids engage in flexible thinking, they are better able to cope with change and new information, both out in the world and within the classroom. What we know is that children who have difficulty with flexible thinking often struggle to take on new tasks and frequently have difficulty solving problems. This can set them up for emotional meltdowns when things don't go the way they think they should.

Weak flexible thinking skills can negatively affect both social and academic development. In the case of reading skills, for example, rigid thinkers can have difficulty understanding the correct pronunciation of words and tend to interpret the text literally. Writing can be a difficult task for young children because it requires several skills. They need to add details, write supporting sentences, and edit for errors. When kids are rigid in their thinking, it can be hard to shift between all these skills. Even math requires flexible thinking. When kids understand there is more than one way to solve a problem, they can shift gears and look for different strategies. If they get stuck in a certain thought process and struggle to try a new approach, math can be very frustrating.

We are bombarded with new information and opportunities to embrace change, and children are no different. This can be overwhelming.

For some children, engaging in rigid thinking is the path of least resistance because it feels safe; for other children, rigid thinking is their go-to because they just haven't developed flexible thinking skills yet.

And *developed* is the key word here. This implies flexible thinking is a skill and it can be taught, learned, and developed.

The good news is flexible thinking skills can be practiced at home. Try a few of these strategies to help your child move away from rigid thinking.

BRAIN STATES AND WHY THEY MATTER

The lizard brain only wants to eat and be safe. The lizard brain will fight (to the death) if it has to, but would rather run away. It likes a vendetta and has no trouble getting angry. The lizard brain cares what everyone else thinks, because status in the tribe is essential to its survival.

—Seth Godin

The human brain is an incredible pattern-matching machine.

—Jeff Bezos

I N THIS CHAPTER WE WILL spend some time discussing the brain and brain states. We discussed the brain and brain development in an earlier chapter. That chapter laid the foundation for this one. However, in this chapter I want to focus not on how the brain develops but on how the brain states affect our behavior.

Now, I am no neurologist and don't want to give the impression I am, by any means, an expert on the brain. However, I find the brain and brain states fascinating, and my interest has led me to explore some brain basics. Having a working knowledge of brain basics has really helped me understand the why behind so much of what people do—and don't do. I find that having a basic understanding of the reasons people do what they do has helped me respond more appropriately to situations and circumstances that are presented to me. It is important to remember all behavior is a form of communication. The person, no matter how young or old, is trying to tell you something with their behavior. Your job, if you choose to accept it, is to try to understand what the person is trying to tell you.

Before we get too far ahead of ourselves, let's look at some brain basics. In chapter 2, we discussed some of the qualities of the brain. It is said that the brain is the most complex part of the human body. We know the brain weighs about three pounds and is the seat of intelligence, the interpreter of the senses, the initiator of body movement, and the controller of our behavior. This all-powerful organ is encased in a bony shell and protected by cerebrospinal fluid. We know that the brain is the source of all the qualities that define us as human. Some say the brain is the crown jewel of the human body. Certainly, the brain is the control center of our bodies, as it controls thoughts, memory, speech, and movement. When the brain is healthy, it works quickly and automatically. Most of us probably don't spend much time thinking about the brain and how or why it works; we just know it is working, and all is well. We also need to keep in mind that we only get one—yep, just one brain—and we need to take care of it. I also believe taking some time to understand some how and why basics of the brain can help us better understand behavior and emotions.

When you do the research about the brain and brain states, there is an overwhelming amount of information. It is easy to become confused and lost in the medical jargon. Here's my suggestion: keep it simple so it can be useful. We can start with the scientific focus of brain states, but honestly, after taking a close look at the neuroscience behind brain states, I found the information very technical and not as useful in my day-to-day life, especially when it comes to helping to manage behavior. The information can be very technical and a bit overwhelming when trying to apply it to everyday life. Sure, it would be great if we could all be in beta (and what the heck is beta?) and have brain waves associated with normal waking consciousness and a heightened state of alertness, logic, and critical reasoning. But let's be real. It ain't happening 24/7, and what we really need are some strategies for dealing with the kid/adult/ person who is not in beta. (By the way, beta is the brain state that would be ideal for most people most of the time.)

Beta is your wizard brain. The difference between a wizard brain and a lizard brain (brainwise-plc.org) is simply a matter of brain state. Wizard and lizard brain suggest there are two basic parts to the brain: the prefrontal cortex and the limbic cortex. I think most can agree with these two parts of the brain and the way they interact in the brain to dictate a person's general state. The wizard brain (prefrontal cortex) is the thinking brain. It tells a person to stop and think before acting. This brain is relaxed and in control. By contrast, the lizard brain (limbic cortex) is impulsive and reactive. The lizard brain is the seat of emotion, addiction, and mood.

OK. I've got some suggestions on this brain state stuff. First, I have to say my years of experience working with children with emotional and behavior disorders have helped me understand the importance of emotional states. I have always been a firm believer that managing my emotions helps others manage theirs, especially when in challenging, emotional situations. In the past eight to ten years, I have become even more convinced that my behavior and reaction has a direct impact on the state of the other person. This has led me to research a variety of approaches/theories/curricula that could help me gain a better understanding of brain state and ways I can help children manage and regulate their emotions. Let me share what I have learned.

My go-to in almost every situation is Conscious Discipline. Conscious Discipline was developed by Dr. Becky Bailey more than twenty years ago and is focused on using what we know about the brain to consciously support our children (and others) in a loving and respectful manner. Conscious Discipline believes we (the adults) must change our behavior and mindset first and then model our expectations for others. The program uses the Brain State Model, the Seven Powers for Conscious Adults, and the Seven Skills of Discipline. For the sake of this discussion, I want to focus on the Brain State Model used in Conscious Discipline, and I encourage you to do your own research into Conscious Discipline. Dr. Bailey has a podcast, YouTube videos, and so much amazing information on her website (https://consciousdiscipline.com).

Dr. Bailey likens behavior to an iceberg. The tip is all you can see; you don't really know what's happening under the water or how large the iceberg really is. So, the behavior you see is only the tip of the iceberg. What is really happening on the inside for the child? What is the child's internal state? We can see the external state, and more times than not, we react to what we can see, never giving a thought to what is happening on the inside that is causing the upset. The focus of Conscious Discipline is to understand the communication behind the behavior instead of just stopping the behavior. Remember, I mentioned before that *all* behavior is communication. What is the child trying to communicate to you?

Conscious Discipline focuses on three brain states:

1. Survival State, brain stem (Always thinks the tiger is chasing them.)

   - Need of the Survival State: safety (Always asking, "Am I safe?")
   - Skills of the Survival State: fight, flight, freeze/surrender

2. Emotional State, limbic system

   - Need of the Emotional State: love (connection) (Always asking, "Am I loved?")
   - Skills of the Emotional State: whatever skills we were taught during our childhood by significant adults when they were stressed, such as yelling, whining, complaining, blaming, name-calling, procrastinating, and so on.

3. Executive State (CEO), brain cortex (prefrontal lobe)

    - Needs of the Executive State: exercise and problem-solving
    - Skills of the Executive State: endless, because when we are functioning from our Executive State", we are able to problem solve, be creative, think more clearly, consider options, be patient, have impulse control, take risks, try new things, learn from mistakes, and so on—we are at our best.

Let's take a closer look at each of the states and how they might look in your child (or other adults).

In the Survival State, it looks like this:

- No eye contact
- Resistance to questions, touch, and understanding
- Tense face and body
- Feels concerned and powerless
- Physical aggression (hitting, biting, kicking, etc.)
- Tantrums (screaming, head banging, etc.)
- Withdrawal (running away, hiding, shutting down, daydreaming, etc.)

Remember, this is the fight, flight, or freeze state, and it can look different depending on the child's or adult's reaction to the situation.

- Fight = hit, kick, spit, push, physical aggression
- Flight = run, hide, scream, withdraw
- Freeze = cry, whine, comply, give in, give up

OK, so what can we do when we come across a person in the Survival State? You need a set of tools. Conscious Discipline recommends NARCS (Noticing, Assertiveness, Routines, Composure, and Safe Place):

- N = Noticing: Verbally state your observation of the child's distress through description.
- A = Assertiveness: Use a voice of no doubt.

- R = Routines: First-then statements or visuals.
- C = Composure: Use breathing strategies.
- S = Safe Place or Safe Keeper: Have a safe space to remain calm.

The next state is the Emotional State, and it can look like this:

- Complaining = "Mom, when are we going to get there?"
- Judgment = "She always gets to sit in the front!"
- Blaming = "He's touching me!"
- Name-calling, whining, and tattling
- Attention seeking
- Relationship resistance
- Clinginess
- Perfectionism
- Social exclusion
- Eye contact and touch are helpful
- Connection, understanding, and power seeking
- Relaxed body

Emotional Thinking gets you:

- Always/never and no one/everyone thinking
- Focusing on the negative
- Fortune-telling, predicting the worst possible outcome
- Mind reading, believing you know what others are thinking
- Thinking with your feelings, believing the automatic story generated during the upset
- Guilt, should, must, have to, or ought to
- Labeling, attaching negative labels to self and others
- Personalizing, it's all about you
- Blaming, you made me, I wouldn't _____ if you didn't _____

While we can see this emotional state in our children, we can also see this in many adults. Conscious Discipline recommends REJECT

(Rituals, Encouragement, Jobs, Empathy, Choices, The School/Home Family):

- R = Rituals: Provide predictability.
- E = Encouragement: Use statements like, "You can do it."
- J = Jobs: Power becomes responsibility.
- E = Empathy: Model this behavior by saying, "You seem_____."
- C = Choices: Say, "You have a choice," in a positive way.
- T = The School Family: Love.

The last state is the Executive State, and it looks like this:

- Willingness
- Empathy
- Reflection
- Conflict resolution
- Problem-solving
- Managing emotions
- Setting goals
- Willing and ready to learn

The Executive State says, "What can I learn?" When we are in the Executive State, we are able to see things from many perspectives. The tools that Conscious Discipline recommends are SPACE:

- S = Solutions
- P = Positive intent
- A = Academic integration
- C = Consequences
- E = Executive skills

You can learn more about Conscious Discipline at consciousdiscipline. com, and I encourage you to explore this approach, as well as other brain based approaches such as Zones of Regulation (https://zonesofregulation. com), Social Thinking (https://www.socialthinking.com), and The Incredible Years (http://www.incredibleyears.com). I have used all of these curricula and approaches at different times and in different situations. You can explore them and find one that resonates with you. If you like it, you are much more likely to live it.

The takeaway from this chapter is that brain state matters, and when dealing with a child in the emotional state, it is *so* important you remain in the Executive State. You have to be able to remain calm and rational. If you lose it, so will they. You want them to download your calm, not your crazy. Bring your positive, calm energy to the situation, and help your child learn to be calm. Calm in the chaos is an unbelievably valuable life skill that must be taught. If you don't do calm in the chaos, then you have to learn first so that you can teach your child. First the adult, then the child. Deep breaths and slow exhales. Brain state matters.

KEEP PUTTING THE PEAS ON THE PLATE

Perseverance is not a long race. It is many
short races one after another.

—Walter Elliot

The greatest oak was once a little nut who held its ground.

—Unknown

You have a choice! You can throw in the towel, or
you can use it to wipe the sweat off your face.

—Unknown

THE GIFT OF PARENTING

I HAVE SPENT MY THIRTY-PLUS-YEAR CAREER as an educator. I have taught both children and adults. Most of my career has been spent working with children with special needs. Some of the children I have worked with have had mild learning disabilities and require only minimal support to reach their full potential. Other children I have worked with have had severe behavior disorders and require intensive support. One thing I have noticed with most of the children I have worked with is they lack perseverance and stamina. (We also call this grit.) They give up so easily and become frustrated and overwhelmed when they can't get it or don't want to do it. More times than not, these are children who have been rescued far too often. They are waiting for someone to come along and fix whatever it is that is making them uncomfortable. Listen. Uncomfortable is real, frustration is necessary, and tears are cleansing. Suck it up, buttercup!

I firmly believe frustration is the door to problem-solving. Yes, be there. Show up to facilitate, but stop saving the day. When we are frustrated with a situation, we must make a choice. We must either throw in the towel or use it to wipe our face and persevere. Sure, we can walk away for a time and them come back to the task. It's the coming back that is the determinant. It's the coming back to complete the task that matters most. We must allow our children, even very young children, to experience some level of frustration so they will learn to keep pushing—keep moving forward. Acknowledge the frustration, offer support and suggestions about ways to solve the problem, and then encourage your child to make the final decision about the situation. The frustration will pass, but the problem-solving lesson will remain.

When I sit in meetings with the parents and caregivers of these children, I outline my yearly goals for their child. My first goal is to help their child develop perseverance and stamina. I want their child to learn to push past the discomfort. I need their child to do what they don't like—to finish a nonpreferred task and to reach the goal even if they don't enjoy all of the process. As far as I can tell, most of us engage in nonpreferred tasks most of the day. Let's be honest, if I could be engaged in a preferred task most of the time, I'd be sitting in a chair in Tahiti, sipping something cold from a glass with an umbrella in it.

So, learning to take the deep breath and keep working is the difference between getting it done and giving up.

As a parent or caregiver, you're going to begin to hear, "I don't want to," as soon as the child has the words. Refusals are nothing new with young children. This is your opportunity to help your child build perseverance and stamina. This is your chance to work on developing grit.

Angela Duckworth's TED Talk on grit went viral in 2013, and her *New York Times* best seller, *Grit: The Power of Passion and Perseverance*, is a must read. Building grit in our children has now made it into our schools, and teachers and administrators are working to build these much-needed skills into classrooms in the hope our children will learn to persevere. For Duckworth, grit means passion *and* perseverance. She says many people leave out the passion and only focus on the perseverance. Duckworth says, "I think that the passion piece is at least as important. I mean, if you are really, really tenacious and dogged about a goal that's not meaningful to you, and not interesting to you—then that's just drudgery." Yes, the passion is important, but even working toward a desired goal can include tasks that are less than glamorous. Nevertheless, we persevere.

Here are a few ideas that can help you help your child develop perseverance and stamina, a.k.a. grit:

- **Help your child find their passion.** While very young children may not have a passion, as children get older, they may show an interest in a particular area or activity. Let your child try lots of different activities. They and you will probably know very quickly if it is an area of interest or if your child could take it or leave it. You can begin this at a very young age. My two-year-old granddaughter started soccer at her preschool. She doesn't want to go. She would rather play with her friends on the playground. Playground, 1–Soccer, 0. Next!
- **Place your child in activities that are outside of their comfort zone.** By encouraging children to engage in

new activities that may be challenging, you help them to develop an I-can-do-anything-I-put-my-mind-to attitude. Duckworth suggests you give your child the opportunity to pursue at least one difficult thing and to make it an activity that requires discipline and practice. The activity doesn't matter as much as the required effort and learning experience that comes with it. Being able to say, "I did it, and I didn't die," is more important than the actual activity.

- **Let your child experience frustration.** As I said earlier, frustration leads to problem-solving, which helps build resilience. It is difficult for us, as parents, to watch our children struggle, but taking risks and struggling are important to learning. Don't allow your child to quit at the first signs of discomfort. Help her determine the next best move and provide a level of encouragement and support your child needs to move forward.

- **Model a growth mindset.** In her 2013 TED Talk, Duckworth said the best way to increase grit in children is to teach and model a growth mindset. The idea of a growth mindset was developed by Carol Dweck, author of *Mindset: The New Psychology of Success.* Dweck found people with a growth mindset are more resilient and tend to push through struggles because they believe hard work is part of the process. Further, they do not believe failure is a permanent condition. The growth mindset is shaped by adults through language and behavior we model for our children. When we offer praise for how smart our children are rather than for how hard they worked, we are suggesting brains lead to success rather than hard work. When we talk positively about mistakes, our children begin to understand mistakes are just part of the process and the mistakes can be overcome.

- **Brainstorm together.** When your child is faced with a difficult task and is struggling, one of the best things you can do is to discourage him from giving up at a low point. Use the opportunity to teach resilience and perseverance. Help your child come up with ways to solve the problem. Offer suggestions, as needed, and lead your child in a positive direction with his solutions. However, allow your child to take ownership of the solution. Children need the opportunity to understand that not all learning is easy and often learning can be challenging, frustrating, and boring. Just because it seems difficult doesn't mean they cannot do it.

- **Teach your child that failing is OK.** We need our children to be able to handle setbacks. Setbacks are just that—setbacks. They are not the end of the world and can be overcome. Sharing your challenges with your child will help them see everyone experiences a setback from time to time, and we just need to keep working to solve the problem and make a comeback. Help your child to look for alternative plans and new ways to see a situation. Show your child you can be flexible in your thinking and sometimes things don't go as we planned. Learning to be flexible and recognize a setback will help your child learn alternative ways to solve problems.

- **Discuss effort and not accomplishments.** In the end, the goal is to develop perseverance and stamina. We want to focus on effort not perfection. When we intervene too often, the message we send to our children is we don't have confidence in their abilities to get the job done. The message we want to send is we will celebrate your hard work and a job well done. We will support you as you attempt something new and hard and frustrating and challenging. We are on your side—on your team. We don't expect perfection, just hard work.

- **Be a gritty parent.** You are your child's model. The best way for children to learn to persevere is by watching you, and believe me, they are watching. Manage your own anxiety about trying new things. Talk about things that are hard for you and the ways you plan to work through those things. Stop trying to control your child's actions and instead move into a coaching role. Use encouraging, supportive language with your child so your talk becomes her talk. Offer support when needed, but help your child work through frustration by looking at the situation from other perspectives.

Just when you are about to give up, take a deep breath and give it one more shot. Building perseverance and stamina are life skills and are often more valuable than IQ. While your children may resist things that seem hard or challenging, if you keep putting the peas on their plates, they may eventually give them a try and decide they like them.

TEACHING CHILDREN TO READ THEIR ENVIRONMENT– USING VISUALS

It has been said that 80% of what people learn is visual.

—Allen Klein

I'm a visual thinker, not a language-based thinker. My brain is like Google Images.

—Temple Grandin

EVERY DAY, WE USE THE signs and symbols (visuals) in our environment to successfully move through the day. The ability to read and use these signs and symbols builds independence. Think about it. We use Google Maps to get us to an unfamiliar location. We use our calendars to ensure we make that important meeting or to manage our day-to-day activities and responsibilities. When we are on the road, and feeling hungry, we look for a familiar sign with a well-known logo and know we will get our burger and fries in no time. From traffic lights to the sign on a public restroom, visuals are absolutely everywhere. Without them, we would miss our stop on the train, order the wrong meal, or wander into the wrong public bathroom.

We all need visuals to move easily through the day. I bet you can think of a time or situation when the environment was poorly marked. Perhaps you were headed to an unfamiliar airport to catch a flight. You may have even been in a rental car you needed to return. As you approached the airport—using your GPS, of course—you began to look for the sign for car rental return. It was not well marked, so you passed it. *Ugh.* Now you had to make the airport loop and go in for a second attempt. That time you made it. Now which rental car company? You found it and pulled in, gathered your belongings, and then began the search for the sign that would lead you to the terminal. You found it and headed to the terminal and checked in. You follow me? The number of visuals we relied on just to make it to the flight is innumerable. From the car rental sign to our seat number, we used these visuals to smoothly move through the experience. If it was poorly marked, it increased anxiety and stress. We can become frustrated, angry, or defeated. And we have reasonably good coping skills. Can you imagine how a child might feel, especially a child with a language or learning delay?

Understanding what will be happening next, where we will be going, and how we are getting there can mean the difference between a good experience and a hard experience. Slow down and start to teach your child to read the environment. You might say to your child, "Don't go in that bathroom. That's for boys, and you're a girl." But how do you know? Oh, you looked at the sign, but did you show the sign to your child so she would begin to recognize the difference between the bathrooms? If you take the time to teach this, she will be able to make this determination on the next trip to the public bathroom. By taking the time to teach, you are building independence.

Visuals also keep us safe and provide boundaries and guidelines. The roads have lines painted on them, so I know where I am supposed to drive. Parking lots have lines, so I know where to put my car. Crosswalks have lines, so I know where to walk as I cross the street, and the crosswalk sign tells me when it is safe for me to cross. It is endless! There are so many visuals we rely on every day. We make the assumption our children will just figure out how all of these visual cues will help them. Honestly, many of them will. However, I firmly believe the sooner we begin to teach our children to read the environment, the more secure and safe they will feel. The ability to read the environment increases independence.

In order to teach the visuals, we have to slow down, take the extra time, and point them out. Take the time while you are driving in the car to point out familiar signs. When you are in a public place, point out the restroom signs, exit signs, and where we wait in line for our turn. All of these visuals will help your children learn to successfully navigate the environment. Visual cues in your day-to-day life are the cues you use without even realizing you are using them. Slow down and take the time to build the visual vocabulary with your children.

BUILDING COMMUNICATION SKILLS

Words are singularly the most powerful force
available in humanity. We can choose to use this
force constructively with words of encouragement,
or destructively using words of despair. Words have
energy and power with the ability to help, to heal, to
hinder, to hurt, to harm, to humiliate and to humble.

—Yehuda Berg

You can change your world by changing your words ...
Remember, death and life are in the power of the tongue.

—Joel Osteen

The most important thing in communication
is hearing what isn't said.

—Peter Drucker

F OR MANY OF US, THE terms *speech*, *language*, and *communication* all sound very much the same; however, these terms all have unique meanings. Let's take a minute and explore each of these terms and the way they relate to young children and their development.

Let's start with speech. *Speech* refers to the action of producing speech or the act of speaking. Someone who has a speech disorder may have difficulty with a specific speech sound or with patterns of words or intelligibility. The person may have trouble making the *r* sound and say *w* for *r*. So, for example, this person may say wabbit instead of rabbit.

Types of speech difficulties include articulation disorders or phonological disorders. The child may need the support of a trained speech and language pathologist (SLP) to assist the child with correcting the speech challenges. It is important to remember that often speech sounds are developmental, and there are clear guidelines for when certain sounds should be spoken by the child. A trained SLP will be able to assist with determining if a child has delayed speech or a speech disorder. It is important to be sure the child is developing speech sounds and patterns related to the developmental timeline so the child can hear and make the sounds correctly. This is important, as it can have a direct effect on the child's ability to hear sounds when they begin the reading process. The child will need to be able to hear and produce the sounds clearly as they begin to develop phonological and phonemic awareness. Monitoring speech development will ensure your child is easily understood by others as they attempt to communicate wants and needs. The trained ear of a mother, father, or other primary caregiver is not the same as being understood by those who do not spend as much time with the child. Clear, articulate communication reduces frustration and allows the child to know they can be understood by others.

Now, let's talk about language. I want to begin by saying that speech and language are *not* the same. They are often confused, and the terms are frequently used interchangeably. I often hear parents say, "My child is in speech, but I don't know why. I can understand everything he says without any problem." The truth is the child is receiving language services, *not* speech. Yes, the parent is correct. The child can articulate the sounds correctly and easily and does not need speech services. However, the child is having difficulty with processing language. He is having difficulty understanding what is being said to him, and it can sometimes appear he is not listening. The not listening can be that the child truly does not understand the language, the vocabulary, or the multiple step directions being given to him. He may have a language delay or disorder, and this would be the reason to see an SLP.

So, what is language, and how is it different from speech? Language refers to the ability to communicate through speech by delivering and receiving meaningful messages. Correct language may include delivering and deciphering the message through reading or hearing. A child with language challenges may not use proper sentence construction or grammar or may have difficulty deciphering complex sentences or thoughts.

There are two types of language: expressive and receptive. Expressive language is the ability to express oneself, and receptive language is the ability to decipher and understand language. Receptive language typically develops first and in very young children. Think about your toddler who cannot yet speak, is still babbling, and doesn't have many, if any, words. If you tell the child to go find their shoes or favorite toy, it is likely that they can understand what you have asked them to do. Single-step direction can be followed by a toddler because the child's receptive language is developing quickly.

Expressive language develops later, and we begin to see our children using words, usually nouns, at around eighteen months. Children with a language delay or disorder often have difficulty with receptive language. They may also have challenges with pragmatics, which is the use of social language. We often find that children on the autism spectrum have significant challenges with pragmatics. They are not able to read the needed social cues that come with language. Language acquisition is very, very important for young children, and adults need to talk to and with children to ensure they have lots of language opportunities.

Finally, let's examine communication. Communication is a very broad category. Communication includes spoken language but also includes many other nonverbal cues that are essential for interacting and communicating with others. It is not uncommon for a child to have proper speech and language and yet still have difficulty communicating. This could be in the form of not understanding sarcasm, gestures, or facial expressions. These are all cues for understanding the meaning of what someone is trying to communicate. Again, we often see children on the autism spectrum exhibit challenges with communication, and they may be identified as having a communication disorder.

When we put speech, language, and commination together, we realize how important the development of these skills can be for a young child. The ability to communicate one's needs and wants is a critical component of any relationship. It is important that the other person be able to understand what is being communicated so that person can choose to support the needs and wants of the one communicating. Communication is particularly important if you are a child and rely on adults for your basic needs and wants. If a child struggles with communication, they can often feel frustrated, and this can lead to unwanted behaviors and can sometimes result in a shut down or a meltdown on the part of the child. For this reason, and many more which we will discuss, supporting the development of communication skills is critical for young children.

They say it takes two thousand times in context before a child can understand a new word—*two thousand* times. That means you have said the word *red* in context two thousand times, and then your child says the word *red*, and you think it's magic. The truth is, you said, "red socks," "red balloon," "red cup," and so on, so now your child knows the color and word *red*.

If you are the kind of parent who truly talks with your child and talks about what you are doing and what you are seeing, your child is hearing hundreds of words each day. That child's vocabulary is growing by leaps and bounds, and they are lucky to be living in an environment that is language rich. Go you! You are getting those words into your child's developing brain each day. It will pay off—I promise. If you are a child who is in an environment that is language deprived, you are much less likely to develop the much-needed strong vocabulary. To take it one step further, we will examine the work done by Dr. Dana Suskind and the thirty-million-word project.

Dr. Suskind's book, *Thirty Million Words: Building a Child's Brain*, examines language acquisition in young children and the consequences of a lack of language opportunities. In a nutshell, Dr. Suskind reviewed the work of Betty Hart and Tom Risley and looked at the language discrepancy between children born into lower socioeconomic status (SES) families versus children who were born into professional families. The findings of Hart and Risley were substantiated by Suskind. Children born to professional families heard thirty million more words by the end of their third year than did children born to lower SES families. Thirty million words. Thirty. Million. Words. It actually has a name. The thirty-million-word gap. And it is a gap that is not easily closed. In fact, for many of these children, the gap only widens as they get older and enter school. Children who hear thirty million fewer words start school behind. They have greater difficulty following directions because they do not understand positional words like *up, on, under, beside, between, beneath*, and so on. These children have smaller vocabularies overall, and their use of social language is impaired. Often, they are talked to and not talked with. It could not be more important for you to talk to your child from day one.

Dr. Suskind's book is an excellent read and will help parents and caregivers gain an understanding of the importance of early language acquisition. She shares her approach, which is: "The 3 T's—tune in, take turns and talk more." I say yes to all of these. Communication skills are critical. Talk to your child; narrate all that you do. Feed their language development. It will pay off in the long run.

SCREEN TIME AND THE USE OF TECHNOLOGY

The earlier we introduce screens the more it affects
the child's brain development and the more likely
they will have trouble managing their addiction
to screens and technology later in life.

—Dr. Laura Markham

It's not just about limiting screen time; it's about
teaching kids to develop good habits in real life
as well as managing their screen time.

—Cynthia Crossley

THE GIFT OF PARENTING

L ET ME BEGIN BY SAYING I think technology is amazing. When I was a child, I remember thinking how cool it would have been to be able to call my grandparents (which was a very expensive long-distance call, so it didn't happen very often) and actually see them when I talked with them. I could only imagine. And now it can be and is done all day, every day. We can see the people we are talking to from all the way across the world—*amazing!* I will also say that is here to stay. It is not going away. It is built into our lives and culture and is next to impossible to avoid.

Technology has made so many things so much easier; there are so many benefits to the technological advances that have been made. However, there are still some challenges we face in terms of managing these technological advances. Most of them, such as cybersecurity, identity theft, and email hacking, are for another type of book. The challenges I want to focus on in this chapter are the ways in which technology, specifically screen time, can affect young children.

I don't know what we ever did before this technology made its debut. All the ways in which I see screens being used with young children often makes me wonder how I ever got anything done. I still had to drive my children around town in the car with no tablet or television in the car. I still had to go to the grocery store with no tablet for my children to watch while I shopped. I cooked dinner, washed clothes, and scrubbed the toilets with only a television and a VCR (and we were the last people I knew to get a VCR). We went out to dinner, as a family, without a device for my children to watch while we ate. My point is, I made it. My children survived and thrived, and so did I. They learned to play outside, socialize with friends, read, and do math. They were and still are good students and good citizens. Was it more difficult to do before technology? I believe that is still up for debate. Until about fifteen years ago, screen time was not a real issue. Heck, the first iPad wasn't introduced until 2010. Let's take a look at what's happening now.

Since 1997, the amount of time kids aged two or younger spend staring at screens has more than doubled (Young 2020). Screens are *everywhere.* You can hardly go into a restaurant without seeing a television (or ten) mounted on a wall somewhere. We have smartphones (a.k.a. minicomputers), tablets, and watches we use all day to manage our busy lives, all with screens. It is almost impossible to avoid screens, so it creates a real challenge to minimize the exposure to screens for our young children. So, what is a parent to do? The best thing to do is what's best for you and your child, understanding the implications of too much screen time. Here is some research, some guidelines, and some suggestions for helping you manage screen time with your child. Remember, you are your child's first and best teacher. Interaction with you cannot be replaced by a screen. Your child needs you and your full attention each and every day.

The American Academy of Pediatrics has developed recommended guidelines for screen time for young children. Here are the latest recommendations:

- For children younger than eighteen months, avoid use of screen media other than video chatting.
- Parents of children eighteen to twenty-four months of age who want to introduce digital media should choose high-quality programming and watch it with their children to help them understand what they're seeing.
- For children ages two to five years, limit screen use to one hour per day of high-quality programs. Parents should coview media with children to help them understand what they are seeing and apply it to the world around them.
- For children ages six and older, place consistent limits on the time spent using media, and the types of media, and make sure media does not take the place of adequate sleep, physical activity, and other behaviors essential to health.
- Designate media-free times together, such as dinner or driving, as well as media-free locations at home, such as bedrooms.
- Have ongoing communication about online citizenship and safety, including treating others with respect online and offline.

So, in a nutshell, no screens younger than eighteen months, and between eighteen and twenty-four months, only high-quality media watching *with* you. For ages two to five, only one hour per day—for the entire day, every day. How many three-year-olds only get one hour of screen time per day? This includes any computer time your child may be getting at school, time in the car watching the tablet, the trip to the grocery store or the doctor's office, and so on. I would agree it can be exceedingly difficult for parents to keep screen time for their preschooler to one hour per day. But it can be done. I promise. You may be asking yourself what the big deal is. Does it really matter and what happens if your child gets more than an hour a day? I'm glad you asked.

Several studies regarding screen time and young children have recently been released, one of which was by the *Journal of the American Medical Association* (*JAMA*). Dr. John Hutton (2019), a pediatrician and clinical researcher at Cincinnati Children's Hospital, conducted research on the impact that screens have on children. The research was focused on examining the association between screen-based activities and academic performance. I find this particularly interesting because many parents use technology because they believe it will help to make their children smarter. The findings of this study would suggest just the opposite. In fact, the article states that, "television viewing and video game playing were inversely associated with the academic performance of children and adolescents. In addition, the negative association between these screen-based activities and academic performance seemed greater for adolescents than for children." This means watching television and playing video games is not the best plan for increasing overall academic performance. I know what you're thinking. You're thinking, *Well, my three-year-old doesn't play video games, and he doesn't really watch TV.* Yes, but does he use your phone to watch YouTube? Does he use a tablet to watch a movie? That's a screen, folks.

Another piece of research published in *MIT Technology Review*, titled "Screen Time Might Be Physically Changing Kids' Brains" (Basu 2019), examines the language and literacy skills of young children and the way screen time may impact these fundamental skills. The study reveals children who spent more time in front of screens had what they called "white matter integrity." What in the world does that mean? White matter? Basically, the white matter of the brain can be thought of as the brain's internal communication network. The integrity of that structure, how well organized the nerve fibers are, and how well developed the myelin sheath is are all directly associated with cognitive function, and it develops as children develop language. Children need healthy white matter. White matter matters! The article suggests that the researchers found there's a clear link between higher screen use and lower white matter integrity in the children that were used for the study. That structural change appears to be reflected in the results of the cognitive test the children took as well, which showed high screen time associated with lower levels of language and literacy skills. Honestly, it makes sense. If you are watching a screen, you are not talking with other people, and engaging with other people helps to develop language and literacy skills.

Here's another bit of information about the effects of screens on our children. Studies have shown excessive television watching is linked to the inability of children to pay attention and think clearly. It is also linked to poor eating habits and behavioral problems. Excessive screen time has also been associated with language delays, poor sleep, impaired executive function, and a decrease in parent-child engagement. "It's known that kids that use more screen time tend to grow up in families that use more screen time," Hutton said. "Kids who report five hours of screen time could have parents who use ten hours of screen time. Put that together and there's almost no time for them to interact with each other. About 90% are using screens by age one," said Hutton, who published a number of studies that used MRIs to research the impact of reading versus screen use by kids. "We've done some studies where kids are using them by two months old to three months old." The leading researcher says, "My motto is 'Screen-free until three'—this at least gets kids to preschool with a solid anchor in the real world, where their basic sense of connection with caregivers and early language skills have solidified."

The bottom line: screen time has an effect on the brain. How much and to what extent are still being researched. If you follow the American Academy of Pediatrics' recommendations, no screens at all less than eighteen months and only an hour a day from two to five years old. If you follow Dr. John Hutton, then kids should be screen free until three. There is no hard-and-fast rule, and this can make your decision challenging. However, the research and recommendations *clearly* suggest we minimize screen time for our children. Find ways for your child to engage in other activities, both inside and outside. Select a preschool that is screen free. Engage your child while shopping; have them become your helper. Sing and use music while in the car or try an audio book. Put down your phone, engage with your child, and work on developing those much-needed language and literacy skills. You will be glad you did!

PRAISE VERSUS ENCOURAGEMENT

Those who are nurtured best, survive best.

—Louis Cozolino

THE GIFT OF PARENTING

I S THERE REALLY A DIFFERENCE between praise and encouragement? Aren't I supposed to use positive praise with my child when they do something right or something good? Is my praise supposed to be specific? Which behaviors do I encourage, and which ones do I praise?

There is a difference between praise and encouragement, and the differences and the effects of each have become more widely studied in recent years. What has been found is there is a long-lasting effect of each, and encouragement is more helpful than praise. So, let's talk about the differences and the way you can increase your use of encouragement while also giving praise when it is due.

It is reasonable to want to provide support to those we love. We want to cheer successes and be empathetic during times when our loved one has missed the mark. As a parent, it just seems natural to want to be there for your child. You want to say, "Good job," and high-five every chance you get. It will make your child feel good and will build self-esteem. Right?

Well, actually, we should be a bit careful about using too much praise and not enough encouragement. Certainly, there is a place for both, but encouragement should be your go-to. There are studies that have shown children who receive encouragement during the formative years are more successful later in life. On the other hand, research is now showing consistent praise can be harmful. Who'd a thunk?

OK, so what's the difference, and how do you know when to do what? Let's talk about this. The dictionary definition of each is below.

encourage

1. To inspire with hope, courage, or confidence; hearten.
2. To give support to; foster.
3. To stimulate; spur.

praise

1. Expression of approval, commendation, or admiration.
2. The extolling or exaltation of a deity, ruler, or hero.
3. Archaic A reason for praise; merit.

We all want our children to have a good attitude and a cheerful disposition. Wouldn't it be great if this were the case all the time? What if our kids were never grumpy and always cooperative? Well, let's be serious. That ain't happening. However, there are some things we can do to help our children be more positive and more willing to work with us instead of against us.

When I was an education student and was learning how to be a teacher, my professors always told me to praise my students as much as I could and to be sure the praise was specific. I am sure this is not new information for many of you. So, being the good student that I am, I listened carefully and put into practice everything I was taught. I was the specific praise queen.

It wasn't until many years later I had a shift in thinking. What I realized is that we, as a culture, really overpraise. We use too much praise and not enough encouragement.

Thinking about this, I must ask myself a serious question: Do I want to encourage competition or build cooperation? Let's be honest. A little (healthy) competition is good. It can be a great motivator, and when children learn they can't always win, they may be inclined to work a little harder, or they will try something else. Teaching children how to be good sports is an important life lesson. Bottom line: competition is real, and most children are already competitive to some degree. They don't need us to encourage competition. With that being said, it becomes more important for us to build a cooperative spirit in our children. Teaching children to cooperate will help them throughout life.

So, how can we support cooperation and minimize competition? Easy. We can use more encouragement and less praise.

Wait. What? Am I saying you should reduce the amount of praise you give your child? Yep, that's exactly what I'm saying. Honestly, we all need to be praised from time to time. We all need to hear how wonderful we are. Having your efforts praised feels good! So, let's look at this a bit closer.

Here's what we know about praise and encouragement:

- One of the main differences between praise and encouragement is praise often comes paired with a judgment or evaluation. It makes the adult the final judge and jury. It's all about the adult's opinion. And that's great if the child is a pleaser, but if not, your efforts are lost. It won't work with children who don't care what you think.

- Praise usually ends with *est*—cutest, smartest, fastest, quietest, tallest, funniest, and so on. This will encourage competition for sure. "Wow, you are the quietest walker." "Hey, what about me? I'm a quiet walker too!" Boom—competition.

- Praise focuses on the actor rather than the act. "You are the best at cleaning up the blocks."

- Praise focuses on the product rather than the process. "You look so handsome in that suit."

- Praise sets the adult as the standard by which everything is judged. It can be discouraging for those not receiving it. Failure to earn praise is often interpreted as criticism.

An alternative to praise is *encouragement*. It refers to a positive acknowledgment response that focuses on a child's efforts or specific attributes of work completed. Unlike praise, encouragement does not place judgment on a child's efforts or give information regarding its value. Encouragement is specific to what the child is doing—the act. Encouragement lets the child know they are on the right track and is moving in the right direction. Encouragement focuses on supporting the steps (process) it takes to get to the end (product).

- Encouragement is specific. "You colored that picture and used lots of colors from your crayon box. You worked on it for almost an hour."

- Encouragement is focused on the child's feelings, not the adult's feelings. "You seem so proud of yourself! You didn't think you could get it all done, but you did!"

- Encouragement focuses on the effort, not the outcome. "I was watching you, and I saw that you were really concentrating. You stayed focused even though there were a lot of distractions."

- Encouragement is based in reality. "You have come a long way. You weren't able to read as many words last week."

Praise is important as long as it is genuine praise. Genuine praise is the loving words that arise spontaneously and warmly from the parent's heart, without the thought of manipulating or controlling a child's behavior. All of our children need to hear genuine praise.

I believe encouragement is more important. We have to help children know they are on the right track, help them to keep moving in a positive direction, and help them try again when they are ready to give up. Encourage as much as you can, and praise from the heart!

SHARING VERSUS TURN TAKING

Children who act like this are not trying to be mean.
Instead, the social skills of turn taking, sharing and
waiting are not part of their behavioral skill set …
Take the time to teach these valuable skills.

—Unknown

To Share:

- To have a portion of (something) with another or others. Example: "He shared the pie with her."
- Give a portion of (something) to another or others. Example: "Money raised will be shared between the two charities."

To Turn-Take:

- The process by which people in a conversation (or a play activity) decide who is to speak (or use the toy) next.
- It depends on both cultural factors and subtle cues.

(I WANT TO START BY SAYING this—again. The *only* way to strengthen a behavior is through practice. If you want it to get better, you have to provide opportunities to practice.)

OK, now that I got that off my chest …

Sharing and turn taking are *not* the same. We use these terms interchangeably. When we do, we confuse our children.

There is a difference between sharing and turn taking, and most of the time, I hear them used incorrectly. Words have meaning, and we need to mean what we say. When we share, there is an emotional response. There is a sense of loss associated with sharing. I must give up something, and I am not going to get it back—ever. Some of us are OK with giving up things we really like. Others (most) are not. I know many grown-ups who have difficulty sharing. When you and I share a cupcake, I have to give up part of my cupcake, and I am not going to get it back—ever. That is hard—really hard because I really like cupcakes.

Taking turns is different from sharing. When we take turns with an item, I know I will, at some point, be getting the item back. It is not gone for good. It means I must *wait* while you have a turn, and then I will have a chance to have another turn. Turn taking is hard too, but it is not as hard as sharing. At least the child knows the item will make its way back to them.

A cookie can be shared; a toy cannot. You will not be cutting the toy in half and giving half to each child. We take turns with the car and with the ball. We do not share them. We take turns with a toy, but typically, I don't take turns with a cookie. If a child is interested in playing with a toy, they should ask for a turn, not for the child to share the toy.

A child does not usually understand the concept of sharing until around the age of five. Young children are way too all about themselves to even begin to understand the concept of sharing. Sharing takes practice, and even though it may be a more abstract concept for toddlers doesn't mean we shouldn't make an effort to teach and model sharing. It is never too early to start, and the more practice, the better. Just don't set yourself up for disappointment by expecting very young children to naturally share. Here are a couple of ideas for working on the sharing skills:

- Work on puzzles together and take turns adding pieces.
- Take turns adding a Lego to your tower.
- Share chores around the house—watering the plants, sweeping the floor, or unpacking the shopping bags.
- Give him things to share with his friends—a special snack for friends or a roll of stickers to pass out.

If we want our children to become good at sharing, we have to be good at sharing. We have to provide a positive example of sharing. Our children are going to need help and support in order to become good sharers. And, most importantly, we cannot expect our children to share everything all the time. I can't even do that, and quite frankly, I don't want to do that. Sometimes, what's mine is mine, and I am not willing to share it.

So, let's shift to turn taking. Turn taking is a life skill. It is a skill that is needed for social success in all environments. Can you imagine if we all decided to go at the same time at the four-way stop? It would be a disaster! We each have to wait our turn. The ability to begin to understand turn taking usually emerges around three and a half or four. Turn taking does not just develop naturally for most children. Many children need to be taught turn-taking skills, and they must be offered many opportunities to practice. The adults can't just assume children know how to turn take.

Teaching turn taking involves several skills such as:

- A social understanding of why we take turns. Social awareness is key.
- Self-regulation skills, and this is also a skill that must be learned.
- What to do when I am waiting. Don't assume children know how to wait or that they know what to do while they are waiting.
- Knowing when to take a turn. When is the other child's turn over, and when will it be the child's turn again?

Just like sharing, taking turns can be hard, even for adults. It can be really frustrating to wait for something you really want or if you are in a hurry. I want you to take a second and think about the last time you waited in line for groceries or gas. Do you remember how you felt when you didn't know how long it would be until your turn? Can you remember a time when you had been waiting for your turn and someone cut in front of you and took your turn? Holy cow, that will work with your emotions. If we feel frustrated in these situations, can you imagine how a young child might feel?

Taking turns is one of the most critical social skills needed in day-to-day life. Turn taking is necessary when it comes to developing friendships, communicating with others, and playing games. We must remember children are not born knowing how to take turns. If we do not teach our children how to take turns, they will continue to play with only their interests in mind and demand turns when they want them. This makes for most unpleasant children. They become pushy and demanding—also known as *brats*. If we want our children to become positive play partners, we must teach the skills of turn taking. A child who knows how to take turns learns a valuable skill about how to make friends, empathize, wait, negotiate, and be patient.

Here are a few ideas that will help teach turn taking:

- **Model turn taking.** Modeling is a great way to teach your children how to take turns. If you are not good at turn taking, it's likely that your child won't be good at it either. They are watching you. Be a good model.

- **Use understandable language.** Make the language of turn taking familiar and understandable for your child. Always use simple language to describe turn taking. It's as simple as: "My turn … your turn." Sometimes you might have to give your child a verbal reminder along with a gentle physical reminder. They may get excited for their turn and try to skip your turn. It happens to all of us. If they try to skip your turn, put your hand on top of their hand and say, "My turn."

- **Use a timer.** A timer can be a useful tool to help monitor whose turn it is, when it starts, and when it ends. Often, children need the visual support to know how much longer and then to transition from their turn to the other person's turn.

- **Teach how to play board games.** Teaching turn taking was much easier when we played more board games. Candy Land and go fish naturally lend themselves to turn taking. Puzzles can also be a great tool to use when teaching turn taking.

- **Use cooperative storytelling.** It is important to find opportunities in your day-to-day life to practice turn taking. Cooperative storytelling is a way to practice turn taking with conversation. The first person starts a story. Then the next person says a sentence that must follow in order to make a story. This is a great way for children to learn to listen to the person doing the talking so that they can add to the story and it will make sense.

It is very important that we remember that sharing and turn taking are skills that are developmental and that they have to be taught. It is not reasonable for us to expect young children to have the skills of sharing and turn taking if we have not provided a proper model or if we have not provided enough practice. It is also necessary that we recognize that children should not be expected to share all of their things all of the time. I don't, and neither do you. Sharing is a choice. Turn taking isn't. I can choose to share my cupcake or not. I would likely choose not. However, I must wait my turn at the bank or the gas station. I don't really have a choice about that. We have to have an understanding of these two concepts before we can teach them. Be sure that you see the difference between the two and then use them, in context, frequently. Be patient with your child and with yourself. We can teach children to be good at sharing and also good at turn taking. It will just take time and practice.

REPLACEMENT BEHAVIORS: ASSUME NOTHING

Fortunately, most human behavior is learned observationally through modeling from others.

—Albert Bandura

Most bad behavior comes from insecurity.

—Debra Winger

The fact is that people are good. Give people affection and security, and they will give affection and be secure in their feelings and their behavior.

—Abraham Maslow

"WHAT ARE YOU DOING?"
"Have you lost your x*&# mind?"
"How many times do I have to tell you not to do that?"

Ever said any of those words (or something close to those) to your child? The truth is, we have all probably said something like this on multiple occasions to our children. We make lots of assumptions about behavior and how our children learn to behave. Previously I gave an overview of behavior, and I focused on the need for us to teach behavior the same way we would teach any other skill. Here, I want to focus on replacement behaviors, how to teach them, and the language you can use to support the teaching of replacement behaviors.

Often, we assume children know how to behave. We assume they know what we expect and will always behave in the expected manner. We assume they know how to behave at home, at school, in public, in church, at a party, in the library, and so on. You get the point. The behavioral expectations in all of the settings listed can be very different. We assume because we have told them what to do and how to behave in different situations that they will just do it—this time, next time, and every other time. If that has been your experience, then you are one of the lucky few. Children—people in general, for that matter—don't usually learn a new skill (behaviors are skills) in the first attempt. It takes practice to learn a new skill or to engage in a new behavior.

The truth is, children, by and large, want to please. Children want approval and positive regard from their parents. Children want to do the right thing. We need to help them do that. When your children are young, you are their first and most important teacher. What are you teaching? Most children learn incidentally. By this, I mean that they learn by watching others, and this means you. They learn good, appropriate behaviors as well as less desirable behaviors. Once they enter preschool or kindergarten, they have a new group of teachers: their peers. More times than not, children will pick up new behaviors and bring them home and try them out with you. You will decide if that is a cute-keep-it behavior or an oh-hell-no behavior. Bottom line, your children are watching everything you do and are learning which behaviors are acceptable, which are borderline, and which are a hard *no*.

When we are teaching and shaping behavior, the most important component is consistency. You *must* be consistent. You *must* follow through. You *must* do the work. If you are not willing to show up and do the work, you will likely have little effect on the behavior. So, let's make and assumption. Let's assume you are invested in helping your child become a good citizen. You want to help your child learn positive, prosocial behaviors. You are willing to do the hard work, and you will be consistent because it is important to you and your child. If these assumptions are accurate, then we are ready to move forward with some strategies you can use to support your child as they learn new behaviors.

One of the biggest mistakes we make is telling our children what *not* to do instead of what *to* do. Here's what I mean: We say, "Don't stand in that chair. Have you lost your mind?" We don't tell them why we think standing in a chair is a bad idea. We don't tell them it can be dangerous. We don't tell them what to do instead of standing in the chair. We don't say, "Let's get the stool instead. It's much safer." We just tell them what *not* to do. You *cannot* assume they know or remember what to do instead of standing in the chair. You *must* tell them what to do instead. We call this a replacement behavior.

A replacement behavior is a behavior you want to teach to replace an unwanted target behavior. Focusing on the problem behavior may just reinforce the behavior, especially if the consequence (reinforcer) is attention. If you are paying attention to it, you are reinforcing it. Offering a replacement behavior will help you to focus on what you want instead of what you *don't* want. It also helps you teach the behavior you want to see in the target behavior's place. It is very easy to just give our children the *don't* behavior. Don't touch that. Don't eat that. Don't put that there. Don't hit your sister. Don't lick that. Gross. Don't say that. The list goes on and on. We don't tell our children why, and we don't replace the undesired behavior.

Let's give it a try:

- **"Don't touch that" becomes:** "Be careful when you touch because it is hot. It will burn your hand, and that will hurt. You will need this hot pad if you are going to touch it, or you will need to ask for help."
- **"Don't eat that" becomes:** "If you eat that, it will make your tummy hurt, and that is no fun. If you are hungry, you can ask for a snack."

- **"Don't put that there"** becomes: "That cup does not belong there. Please put it in the sink."
- **"Don't hit your sister"** becomes: "When you hit, it hurts. You need to use your gentle hands. Let's try again."
- **"Don't lick that. Gross"** becomes: "That is not food and is not for licking. It is dirty and can make you sick. Let's rinse out your mouth to keep you safe."
- **"Don't say that"** becomes: "Your words can hurt someone's feelings. You need to use kind words. Let's try again."

I know, I know. It's a lot of words, and it's easier to just say, "Don't do that!" But how many times do you have to tell your child not to do something? In the grand scheme of word count, I am willing to bet you have said, "Don't do that," more times than you care to think about, and the behavior continues. Nothing has changed. You just say, "Did you hear what I said? How many times do I have to tell you to stop doing that?"

You guys, you have to teach the replacement behavior. They don't know what you want them to do. They just know you don't want them doing *that*, whatever *that* is.

Remember, you get more of what you focus on. If you want more of gentle hands, then focus on gentle hands. If you want more of walking feet, then focus on walking feet. It is a shift in thinking and will be difficult at first. You will have to make some changes in your language and tell your child the reason you want a particular behavior and then reinforce that behavior. If you are consistent and take the time to teach, the results will be worth it. I promise.

STOP STATEMENTS
VERSUS
START STATEMENTS

REQUESTS
VERSUS
COMMANDS

When you wake up every day, you have two choices. You can either be positive or negative; an optimist or a pessimist. I choose to be an optimist. It's all a matter of perspective.

—Harvey Mackay

" **S** TOP TOUCHING YOUR SISTER."
"Stop screaming."
"Stop throwing the blocks."
"Stop! Just stop!"

Most of us spend a good bit of our time telling our children to *stop*. The thing about telling our children to stop is it really won't change the behavior. It might interrupt the behavior for a moment, but the behavior is likely to return and be as strong as ever. Of course, there are times when *stop* is necessary. I am not suggesting you should not ever tell your child to stop. Certainly, if your child is in danger or is going to hurt herself or someone else, *stop* is necessary. However, when your go to is a stop statement and not a start statement, you probably won't see any significant changes in your child's behavior.

You see, telling a child to stop a behavior will do just that: stop it. (If you're lucky.) It will stop the behavior for the time. It's a temporary fix. It is not a solution. When our children are misbehaving, we want the behavior to stop. Misbehavior is no fun, and it can be embarrassing and very frustrating. We think by getting the behavior to stop, it will somehow magically go away and never, ever return. Wouldn't that be nice? If you believe this, I've got some oceanfront property in Arizona I could sell you. It ain't likely to happen.

We assume children know what to do instead of misbehaving. We frequently say things like, "You know better than that," or, "You know how to behave." We tell them to stop doing something but don't tell them what they can do or should be doing instead. We believe because they know how to behave, they will automatically exhibit the expected behavior. What if they don't? What if they forgot? What if they need more practice with what they should be doing? What if they are misbehaving to get your attention? If this is the case, the stop statement will not be helpful to them and will probably only frustrate you.

So, then what can be done? We have to figure out a way to manage this misbehavior. My vote is to try start statements. Using start statements instead of stop statements can help in several ways. First, let's talk about what a start statement is. A start statement is used to tell a child what they can do instead of what they can't do. Instead of saying, "Stop yelling," we say, "You are too loud. You need to use your inside voice." You might say, "You may not stand in the chair. Chairs are for sitting. You may sit in the chair." I believe it is important to point out the behavior you want the child to stop and then offer the appropriate replacement behavior. The most important part of a start statement is to offer the replacement behavior. With start statements, you are focused on the behavior you want rather than the behavior you don't want. Stop statements focus on the behavior we don't want. "Stop running," is focused on running. "Stop yelling," is focused on yelling. And, "Stop hitting," is focused on hitting. Remember, you get more of what you notice. What you feed will likely grow. Focus on the behavior you want instead of the behavior you don't want.

Start statements will offer the child the replacement behavior and will let you know if the child really does know what to do instead. If, by chance, the child is unsure of what to do, your start statement will clear that right up. By telling the child what to do instead of what not to do, you are sure they have been given the expected behavior. If they don't engage in the expected behavior quickly and correctly, it gives you the opportunity to teach—yep, teach. You may actually need to teach the appropriate behavior.

Start statements will encourage a positive interaction between you and your child. Instead of focusing on the negative, inappropriate behavior, you will have the opportunity to focus on those positive, more desirable behaviors. Paying attention to the behaviors you want rather than the ones you don't want will strengthen your relationship with your child. Your child is looking for your attention. The type of attention you give your child is up to you, and this attention will drive the types of interactions you have with your child. These interactions can either be positive or negative. Don't get me wrong. There will be times when your interactions will not be positive. It happens. We just want to have more positive than negative. Start statements will give you the opportunity to increase the positive behavioral interactions with your child.

This seems like a good time to also talk about the difference between a request and a command. Now I am a firm believer in both a request and a command. However, they are certainly not the same and should not be used as if they are. I cannot tell you how many times I hear parents using a request when they should have used a command. Then the parent becomes frustrated and angry when the child does not comply with a request. By definition, a request is an act of asking politely or formally for something.

Commands help us to enforce rules and limits. Let me be a bit more specific. A request gives the child the option to say *no*—or *yes* if they are feeling compliant. For example, you may say, "Honey, can you please pick up the Legos?" This request would allow your child the option to say, "No." If the child does indeed need to pick up the Legos, then a request was *no* the way to go. It allowed your child to opt out, and now let the power struggle begin. You will now begin to talk too much.

It will probably go something like this: "It's time to go, so you need to pick up the Legos."

"No, I am still playing with them."

"Well, we need to go, so let's get them picked up."

"No. I'm not ready." Crying begins.

The parent is embarrassed and frustrated, so the parent begins to pick up Legos, and child cries louder and tries to take the Legos out of container. A hot mess is happening now.

When the child does not follow your request, you're probably going to become angry and frustrated, and additional requests will follow the initial request until you finally give a command. Here's a piece of advice: start with the command and avoid the multiple requests that will likely come.

Commands help you set limits, and the goal in setting limits is to strike a balance between using enough commands to maintain some control over behavior while allowing children to develop and exercise self-control in other areas. Before giving a command, think about whether this is an important issue and whether you are willing to follow through with a consequence if the child does not comply. Here are some additional things to think about regarding commands:

- Don't give unnecessary commands.
- Give one command at a time, especially with young children. Allow the child to comply with the first command before moving on to the next one.

- Be realistic in your expectations and use age-appropriate commands. Give commands you know the child has the skills to do. Don't set the child up for failure.
- Use commands that clearly detail required behaviors. Be specific about the behavior you want from the child. Instead of saying, "Just a minute," say, "Wait five minutes, and then I will play with you." "Wait a minute," "Be careful," "Be nice," "Knock it off," and, "Watch out," are all vague and can be confusing.
- Use start statements.
- Give children the opportunity to comply.
- Give warnings and helpful reminders.
- Use when-then or first-then statements. Avoid if-then statements, which are requests.
- Give children choices when possible. Teach choice making.
- Make commands short and to the point.
- Praise compliance or provide consequences for noncompliance.
- Teach and encourage problem-solving with children.

Just say it like you mean it: "It's time to pick up your toys. You need to put them away now." If you think it sounds mean, then add a *please* in there somewhere. My point is, if you start your statement with *can you*, *could you*, or *would you*, that is a request. "Can you put on your shoes?" is a request. What you really mean is: "It's time to put on your shoes." Say what you mean, and you are likely to avoid multiple requests that ultimately lead to a command.

Commands are very important. We need to give clear, concise commands to our children. By definition, a command is to give an authoritative order. With that being said, too many commands at one time can be very confusing. Keep your commands to a minimum. It is said a child with perceived misbehavior hears eighty commands an hour. That's crazy! No one wants to hear eighty commands in an hour. However, commands are important so your child is clear about your expectations. Yes, you will seem a bit bossy, but you are the boss, right?

I mean, if you aren't in charge, who is? Someone has to be, and I don't think it should be your young child. Be a little bossy. Be clear with your commands, and balance them with your requests.

For me, using start statements and commands gives children a very clear picture of the expected behavior. Saying, "Chairs are for sitting. You may sit in the chair," is a positive way to tell a child to sit down in the chair. It is the complete opposite of saying, "Don't stand in the chair." It is also the opposite of saying, "Honey, can you sit down in the chair please?" I am not asking you to sit in the chair. I am telling you this is the behavior I expect. Give it a try, and see if you notice a change in your child's behavior. If you are typically a stop statement request-giving parent, this will take some practice. Your child will also have to get used to the change. Be patient with yourself and with your child. It works. I promise.

TEACHING EMOTIONAL REGULATION: IT'S OK TO HAVE A HARD DAY!

Do not teach your children never to be
angry; teach the how to be angry.

—Lyman Abbott

Children learn how to regulate their emotions through
"co-regulation." The better we can soothe them when
we are agitated, or support them when they are low, the
better they "absorb" how to do this for themselves.

—Dr. Stuart Shanker

I WANT TO START THIS CHAPTER by saying that every once in a while, we all have a hard day. I prefer to say *hard* rather than *bad*. I also like to help children see the *good* parts of the day and understand the whole day probably wasn't *hard*. Far too often, we forget children are people too. They are just shorter, less skilled versions of us. If we can have a hard day, then so can they. So, when they struggle with an activity, a request, or at an event, cut them some slack. They have to be allowed to have a hard day too. Give them a hug, help them up, and focus on the good parts of the day.

With that said, let's talk about emotional regulation. Kindergarten teachers will tell you a child's ability to self-regulate is more important to them than the child's knowledge of readiness skills like the ABCs and 123s. You know why? It is because a teacher can teach a child who can manage their behavior. It is very difficult to teach a child who can't sit still, who can't attend, and who is unkind and unwilling. The ability to manage one's behavior and emotions can mean the difference between a good day and a hard day.

Emotional regulation is a person's ability to provide adequate control over their emotional responses to particular situations. Emotional dysregulation refers to someone whose anger and aggression keep them from making and keeping friends, or the child whose withdrawal from emotional challenges leads to avoiding any new activity. It is important to remember emotional regulation is developmental. The younger the child, the more challenging emotional regulation can be. It takes practice to manage your emotions, especially the big emotions. Just like walking, talking, and toilet training are developmental steps, emotional regulation is a developmental achievement that is not present at birth. It *must* be *learned*. If it must be learned, then someone has to teach it. That someone is probably you. However, if you aren't so great at regulating your emotions, you should probably find someone who is and let that person teach your child. You can't teach a skill you don't have. The first step is admitting that this is a skill that is not in your wheelhouse.

At first, regulation must be provided by the environment. If the child has a wet diaper, they cry because they need outside help to reduce the internal tension. The parent helps by trying to understand the meaning of the child's cry and takes action to calm the child. We all know that some babies are easily calmed, and others are more difficult. This would suggest that infants are born with individual differences in their abilities to self-regulate. It also suggests that your response will differ depending on the child's temperament. In toddlerhood and in the preschool years, the child's emotional regulatory system starts to mature and the burden of emotional regulation begins to shift from parent to child. The parent continues to act as an emotional coach.

As the emotional coach, you are working to help the child develop an emotional vocabulary and understand that emotions are real and OK. The emotion is not what gets us into trouble; it is the reaction to the emotion that can cause us problems. As the coach, you help the child recognize and label the emotion. For example, your child really wanted to go outside and play, but this morning it is pouring down rain. Your child asks to go outside, and you tell him that he can't go out because it is raining. He begins to cry and drops to the floor. Is he sad? Is he disappointed? These are not the same emotions. Help your child understand the difference by labeling the emotions correctly. Then, help your child decide the best way to handle the reaction to the emotion. This will help them to develop the regulatory skills that they will need. It is important to remember that emotional regulation is directly tied to language development. As children begin to develop language skills, they become increasingly able to label their emotions, thoughts, and intentions, which helps them regulate their emotional responses. With increased language skills, children are better able to let their parents know what they need in order to calm themselves. Remember, young children still need their parents to help them regulate intense (big) emotions. It only stands to reason then that if a child has a language delay or disorder, it is likely that child will have difficulty with emotional regulation. Also, very young child who do not yet have language will struggle with emotional regulation.

Research suggests that at least three processes underlie children's growing ability to regulate their emotions:

- Neurological maturation: The growth and development of the child's nervous system provides the hardware required for controlling emotional reactions.

- Temperament and developmental status: Some children are more vulnerable to emotional dysregulation due to learning difficulties, language delays, attention deficits, or difficult temperament.
- Parental socialization and environmental support: Differences in how families talk about feelings (their own and others) are related to later differences in the ways children express their feelings and regulate their emotions.

While I believe it is important to be your child's emotional coach, I also feel strongly that we should avoid putting words in our child's mouth in terms of labeling their emotions. By this, I mean when your child begins to cry, don't say, "Oh, you are sad. You are crying." How do you know they are sad? I mean, I cry when I am sad, mad, frustrated, scared, and so on. Stick to the facts. Just notice aloud: "Oh my, you are crying. Something happened. Can you tell me or show me what happened?" Then we can try to determine the source of the crying, and then we can attempt to label the emotion. Perhaps the child is crying because it's raining: disappointment. Perhaps they can't put on their shoes: frustration. Perhaps they got their finger caught in the dresser drawer: pain. Perhaps there was a loud clap of thunder: scared. Do you see what I mean? Your response as an emotional coach will differ based on what happened. A loud clap of thunder = crying = "Oh boy, that was a big noise. A big noise can be scary, but I am here, and you are safe." A rainy day = crying = "You are disappointed because you wanted to go outside. Let's think of some fun things to do inside until the rain stops." Different emotions require different responses to help your child develop emotional intelligence and emotional regulation.

Don't send your child onto the field of life with poor emotional regulation skills. Poor emotional regulation makes it difficult to get along with others and will, undoubtedly, impact the child's overall success. Coach them well, and coach them early. It will pay off.

LIMIT SETTING, RULES, ROUTINES, AND RITUALS

Routines give them a sense of security and help them develop self-discipline. Parents can help kids to feel safer and secure by consistently maintaining rules at home. Rituals are an expression of unity. All cultures create rituals. They are sacred spaces designated for togetherness and connection.

—Dr. Becky Bailey

R ULES KEEP US ALL SAFE, routines help us know what is coming next, rituals keep us connected, and limits tell us what we can and can't (shouldn't) do. All are important, and most of the time, we put them in place without really thinking about it. We establish rules and routines and set limits for our children without taking the time to think about the why. Many times, we just do. What's worse is that we often forget to tell our children the why of the rule or limit. Sometimes we just say, "Because I said so," and expect this will be good enough for our children. I get it. You're the adult, and that makes you the boss. I mean, someone has to be in charge, and it probably shouldn't be your three- or four-year-old. But let's take a minute and step back and talk about how we can establish healthy limits, positive rules, predictable routines, and quality rituals.

The reality is some of us are rule followers by nature, some are rule breakers, and some are rule benders. All of us fall into one of these categories when it comes to rules, including your kids. I have two children. One is a black-and-white, rule-following child. The other is a very gray child who is a true rule bender. Neither of my children ever really broke the rules. But one of them frequently bent the hell out of the rules. I believe you see these traits emerge early in children.

Does your child push the boundaries? Does your child generally comply easily with your requests and commands? Do you frequently have to redirect your child? And how do you handle it when you get pushback from your child? Your responses and reactions are critically important regarding limit setting and rules. Regardless of the category you fall in or your children fall in, what we know for sure is limits and rules are important for your children. Rules are just part of life, and having guidelines helps kids learn how to manage in different situations. Rules provide the framework for children to understand what is expected of them at home, with friends, and at school. While parents know this kind of structure is important, it's often challenging to establish and maintain rules at home.

With regard to rules and limit setting, I have a few suggestions. First, think about the rules that are your nonnegotiables. These are the rules that are set in stone. You will not bend on these rules under any circumstances. One of my nonnegotiables is you will wear your seat belt in the car or you will sit in your car seat in the car. This is a safety issue and is not open for discussion—*ever.* You may only have two or three nonnegotiables. You will need to teach these to your child, and you must enforce them consistently if you want any credibility. If you bend on these rules, you lose credibility, and your children may push you on other rules. So, start by thinking about your nonnegotiables and put them on your rules list. Next, come up with four to five other rules you would like to be sure your children know. These are your general household rules.

For example, it may be important to you that your children put their clothes in the hamper when they undress, or maybe you want your children to clear their places at the table when they are finished eating, or maybe it's that they wear their shoes when they go outside. Whatever it is, establish it as a household rule and then *teach* the rules. Don't just assume your children will know and understand the reason for the rule. You will have to take the time to teach the rules and help your children understand the reason the rule is needed and important. For many children using warnings, providing alternatives, and involving children in problem-solving are effective strategies for encouraging cooperation and compliance with established rules and limits. It is also important to note distractible children need warnings, reminders, and redirection. This is also good advice for young children, as they have short attention spans. As always, adults should monitor their use of the word *no.* Give a *no* only when it is necessary. Use a conditional *yes* instead.

For example, your child is asking for a cookie before dinner. You have a choice of response. You can say, "No you can't have a cookie; you haven't eaten your dinner." This response is likely to lead to upset, which can be crying, screaming, or having a tantrum. Now your child is disrupted, and so are you. The other possible response is, "Yes, you can have a cookie as soon as dinner is finished. I will put your cookie on this napkin and leave it on the counter for you for after dinner." You have used a conditional *yes.* You are teaching delayed gratification, and your child sees you validate his want and take the time to acknowledge the request with a yes. Likely, you will get a more compliant child.

Here's another example: Your child asks, "Can I have a snack?" And the adult responds, "No, you haven't washed your hands." The child only heard *no* and is now crying. The adult will now try to convince the child that if they had been listening, they would know all the child needs to do was wash their hands. For heaven's sake, what is the problem?

Now imagine the same scenario, but this time, the adult says, "Yes, you can have a snack as soon as you wash your hands." Again, this is a conditional *yes*. The child yells, "Yay!" and runs to the sink to wash his hands. Which child do you want to deal with? Just say *yes* as often as you can.

There are times when parents may refrain from establishing rules and limits. This can occur because parents feel guilty about putting too many rules on their children, parents don't want to fight the battles that may ensue when kids object to a rules or limit, or parents don't want to deal with children's temper tantrums when they can't have their way. But children need boundaries and limits to feel safe and secure. Despite what children might say, these guidelines are good for them. By setting limits, parents teach kids important skills that will help them succeed in all areas of life.

So, if children need rules and limits, why do they test them—daily? There are a few reasons your children may test the rules, limits, and you. First, your children may test to express their individuality. They may also test to express autonomy. They each want to be their own person and don't appreciate being told what to do. Too bad, pumpkin, you're not driving *this* train. You are not in charge here. They may also test the rules and limits to determine if you will be consistent. Do you really mean what you say? Are you going to throw in the towel and let them win this battle? Only by bending or breaking a rule can children determine whether it is actually a rule or a one-time command. Only consistent limit setting will teach children the expected behavior. Some children have learned if they protest long enough and hard enough, they can get what they want. Be prepared for testing! Don't take it personally!

Do you value routine? Does a predictable, regular routine make you feel stressed or relaxed? Do you feel upset when the routine is off? Do you work hard to maintain the same routine with your child? Are you a fly-by-the-seat-of-your-pants kinda person? The challenge is that if you are a fly-by-the-seat-of-your-pants kinda person and your child craves structure and routine, you will likely have some challenges. And if you are a super-duper rule and routine follower and your child is a loosey-goosey kinda kid, getting out the door in the morning will be a challenge on the regular. Lord help you in the face of: "Hurry up, and let's get moving!"

Routines support your rules and limits. Routines help children know what is coming next. Routines make the world predictable and safe. Routines reduce anxiety because your children know what is coming next.

So, what is a routine? A routine is a repeated, predicable event that provides a foundation for daily tasks in a child's life. Routines are events that regularly occur in a certain order. Routines help children learn the order of what happens during the day and understand what comes next. Routines are how we teach expected behavior. Routines are similar to blueprints that are used to build a house or building. Routines tell others what is expected, where, and when by providing consistency and predictability. Routines include the order of events for getting ready to go to school in the morning. A routine can be bath time and bedtime. Young children quickly learn routines as long as they are consistent and predicable.

From routines, we develop rituals. Rituals are an expression of unity. Rituals hold families together. Rituals provide ways for us to connect with each other. So, what is a ritual? A ritual is a special action that helps us navigate emotionally important events or transitions in our lives, as well as enhances aspects of our daily routines to deepen our connections and relationships. A ritual is a procedure or routine that is infused with deeper meaning. Rituals help make common experiences uncommon events.

Maybe you have a bedtime ritual and sing the same song to your child each night before they go to sleep. Many of us have holiday rituals. Daily rituals occur day after day in the same place, at the same time, and for the same reason. This will build connection and trust with your children. Without trust, children are not likely to relax their defenses enough to allow you to guide them. Without guidance, you will not be able to discipline your children and likely will not gain cooperation. Remember, as Dr. Becky Bailey states in her book *Conscious Discipline,* connection equals cooperation. In the end, what we want most is cooperative, connected children.

REGULATION STATION
VERSUS TIME-OUT

"Self regulation is a skill, so let's teach it. Kids
aren't born with it any more than they're
born knowing how to tie their shoes."

—grattefulmind.com

"When little people are overwhelmed by big emotions,
it's our job to share our calm, not join their chaos."

—L. R. Knost

THE GIFT OF PARENTING

SELF-CONTROL—THAT'S THE GOAL. KEEP IT together. And if you can't, there's always time-out. Time-out has become our solution when children can't seem to manage their own behavior. When the child is noncompliant, insubordinate, belligerent, disrespectful, or a *brat*, they are going straight to time-out. Time-out is the parents' solution to all that is wrong with the child. We even say things like, "Do you need to go to time-out?" Really? Is that a *real* question? Do we expect the child to respond? Are you waiting for your three-year-old to say, "Why yes, I think a time-out would be just what I need at this moment"? Don't ask. Tell. Say something like, "I see you are having a hard time right now. Let's take a break."

So, let's take a minute and talk about time-out. What is it really? Why should we use it, and when is it most appropriate? Time-out came to be about thirty years ago as a method to help parents become more positive, proactive parents. Time-out could be used instead of spanking. Both parents and children needed a break, and time-out could give this break. The child could calm down, and so could the parent. No more hitting a child in a fit of anger. Sounds like a great plan to me. Hitting children to tell them not to hit always seemed like a terrible idea to me. So, parents decreased spanking (*yay*) and increased giving time-outs. On the surface, this sounds like a great idea. The problem we have is time-out has become a form of punishment. It is overused or used incorrectly. And then we ask children if they want or need to go to time-out.

In its purest form, time-out is just that—time-out. It's time spent away from the source of the problem, time spent away from the reinforcing activity, and time spent away from the attention of the parent or peer. It was supposed to be a break away. Time-out really means time out from any attention. Many parents have found time-out to be more effective in improving behavior than hitting, yelling, and threatening. Time-out has been shown to be effective in decreasing various problem behaviors such as temper tantrums, not following directions, and acts of aggression. Time-out is a great plan when a child has engaged in an act of aggression and needs to be reminded that hitting, spitting, and/ or kicking will *not* be tolerated.

Time-out can be a very effective tool to manage the behavior of young children. The critical component is that it must be delivered with consistency. It is important to decide which behaviors will get the child sent to time-out. It is recommended there only be one or two behaviors focused on as you begin to use time-out. For me, without a doubt, any act of aggression is an immediate time-out. Do not pass go. Do not collect two hundred dollars. Just go. And please, don't talk about it. "You hit. Hitting hurts. Go to time-out." So then, acts of aggression and what? This should be any other one or two behaviors you deem absolutely nonnegotiable. It will be easier to manage, and you will have a greater success rate if you eat the elephant one bite at a time.

Be consistent. Children need to know you are serious about extinguishing behaviors you see are inappropriate and nonnegotiable. Once those behaviors are under control, move to other challenging behaviors and begin to work on those. As soon as the child displays the behavior, move the child to time-out. Don't wait, and don't negotiate. Be consistent. When the child is quiet, start the time. How long should they sit in time-out? Does it really matter? The general rule is one minute for each year the child is old—for example, three minutes for a three-year-old. Guess what? Three-year-olds can't tell time, so they won't know it's been three minutes. My point is that it really doesn't matter. The point is to make the child successful. If the child goes to time-out and is sitting quietly for thirty seconds, take it and move on.

Is it reasonable for a three-year-old to be expected to sit quietly for three minutes? What are you hoping to achieve? If the child is sitting quietly for one minute, you can decide to reinforce by saying, "Thank you for sitting quietly. Now let's try that again." Don't get locked in to the minute-per-year-old thing. The behavior needs to be interrupted or redirected. If that can be done in thirty seconds, then take it and move on to more positive interactions with the child. Time-out should not be used as punishment. If the child needs a consequence for a behavior, then that consequence should follow the time-out. Remember that time-out is just that—time away.

Remember that all children have moments.

Time-out was never intended as the be-all and end-all of discipline. Parents need a big bag of tricks. If you are putting all of you discipline eggs in the time-out basket, you will be stuck. It *will not* work every time.

You need more strategies that can include redirection (interrupting a tantrum in progress with distractions like saying, "Look at that fire truck!") and prevention (cutting short a trip to the grocery store before the child has a moment and the trip becomes negative). You also need to have what is called time-in. Are you spending quality, positive time with your children? Are you building that positive bank account of positive reinforcement? As parents, we have to catch our children being good. When your children are displaying positive, appropriate behavior, get in there and let them know. Listen, we all like to hear how well we are doing. That positive feedback keeps us moving in the right direction. The same is true for our children.

Remember, you get more of what you notice. What are you paying attention to? What are you noticing? If you are focused on the negative, you will likely get more negative behavior. If you are focused on the positive, appropriate behaviors, guess what? You are going to get more positive behaviors. Attention is attention, and we all want it to some degree. Children will take what they can get. If you feed the positive, it will grow! I promise.

Be careful what you're feeding. It has a tendency to grow.

Okay, so now let's talk about what I call a *regulation station*. While time-out is usually administered by the adult, I see the regulation station as a tool for the child. Initially, the parent will be there to facilitate the use of the regulation station; however, it is the hope that the child will learn to use it on his own.

Here's the idea behind the regulation station: Truth be told, most people need to move to calm or regulate. Think about it. When you are emotionally upset, do you find a chair in the corner and go there to sit? No, you don't. If you are a runner, you are probably going for a run. A long walk can also be helpful when we are upset. Sometimes we look for a rocking chair or a front porch swing. When we are moving, we are breathing, and breathing will help us to calm. The crazy thing is we send small children to chairs in corners all the time, and then we tell them to calm down. It really is kinda crazy. So, if we can agree that moving helps us calm, then we need to find a way to help children calm down by moving.

The regulation station should help with this. You know your

children. Do they like to pace or rock or crash into a beanbag chair when they are upset? Sometimes they roll around on the floor. Your regulation station could have bubbles or feathers for blowing. It could have a pinwheel or a relaxation bottle. It could have a rocking chair or a beanbag or both.

The point is this space is a space for calming down. It is a space to take a break *before* one of your children falls apart. It is a space the child can go to when they need a moment. The child is not being punished. The child is not in trouble for feeling—you know, for having emotions. It is OK to be upset and to say, "I need a break."

If you can help your children ask before behaviors escalate, you are being proactive. You are getting in front of the behavior and avoiding possible negative outcomes. Learning to self-regulate is a life skill that will serve children well. As a parent, you have to support your children's emotional needs and teach them to manage their responses to the emotions. Time-out is not always the answer. Sometimes all they need is a break, not a consequence.

TEACHING A CALMING STRATEGY

The ideal of calm exists in a sitting cat.

—Jules Renard

Stop trying to calm the storm. Calm
yourself, the storm will pass.

—Tiny Buddha

When our little people are overwhelmed by big emotions,
it's our job to share our calm, not join their chaos.

—L. R. Knost

"W HEN HE LOSES IT, SO DO I!"

"I just don't know what to do when she starts to scream. I want to spank her, but I know it won't help."

"If you don't stop crying, I'm going to give you something to cry about."

Sound familiar? We have all had those moments when our children are falling apart, and we feel helpless. We just want them to get it together. Often, we resort to saying something like, "You need to calm yourself down this minute!" Or, "Get yourself together right now!" The truth is, at this moment of falling apart, the last thing our kids can do is get themselves together.

I know. You're thinking, *Oh, that's just great. What are we supposed to do now?* It's so embarrassing when a child has a meltdown in public. Everyone stops to look at the show, and then they judge. Oh yes, they judge. They judge the child, and then they judge the parent. They are pretty sure they would know exactly what to do and that the parent is dealing with a spoiled brat of a child the parent has created. You know, karma—she's a bitch! Well, I would say, more times than not, this is *not* the case. This is not a brat of a child, and the parent really is doing their best. The truth is, children have challenges just like anyone else, and the challenges can occur at any given time and in any given place. Further, children don't usually care where, when, or who is watching. The problem is that children have fewer coping skills, and when things don't go their way, the result is usually what I like to call a come-apart. They just come unglued, fall apart, lose it, and become irrational. You know, they have an episode.

The best of children have their moments, and it has to be OK for them to have a hard day. I say *hard*, not *bad*. The day is not *bad*, but there may have been moments that were hard. We have all had a hard day, and our children are no different. What we have to do is help them through it. Learning to stay calm when things don't go your way is a life skill, and for some of us, it can take a lifetime to learn it. For this reason, the sooner we start to teach children to self-regulate and learn a calming skill, the better.

Think of the sitting cat. Even for those of you who don't really care for cats, you can certainly appreciate their calm. They are so patient, so collected. Cats never really seem to fall apart. They never seem to lose it. This is what we want to achieve—the calm in the chaos. We need to teach our children to be like the cat: calm, cool, collected, and rational. OK, OK, I know it's a crazy dream, but we can work on it. It would certainly beat the excited puppy that pees on the floor when they see you. That is not what we are going for here.

When we think about helping children to calm when they are upset, what we are really doing is teaching them to self-regulate. We are teaching children to regulate their emotions. Emotional regulation is more important than most of us realize. There is growing evidence that many children, especially those at risk, begin school lacking self-regulation skills, which may have a great impact on how well they do in school and later in life. There is also evidence that would suggest early self-regulation levels have a stronger association with school readiness than do IQ or entry-level reading or math skills, and they are closely associated with later academic achievement. This is primarily because the ability to remain calm, pay attention, and engage are necessary skills for children to learn. Kindergarten teachers rank self-regulation as the most important competency for school readiness. At the same time, these teachers report many of their students come to school with low levels of self-regulation.

This means we can't wait until children are five or six to begin to help them learn the skills of self-regulation. We have to teach that calming strategy early. How early? As early as possible.

What we know for sure is emotions can be fleeting, persistent, powerful, complex, and even life changing. Emotions can motivate us to act in particular ways and give us the tools and resources we need to interact meaningfully in our social worlds.

Children who ...

- have an answer for everything ...
- have a short fuse ...
- are headstrong ...
- are frequently emotional ...
- are hardheaded ...

... worry us.

Emotional regulation refers to a person's ability to understand and accept their emotional experience, to engage in healthy strategies to manage uncomfortable emotions when necessary, and to engage in appropriate behavior (for example, attend classes, go to work, and engage in social relationships) when distressed. People with good emotional regulation skills are able to control the urges to engage in impulsive behaviors (such as self-harm, reckless behavior, or physical aggression) during emotional distress. These individuals also have a good calming strategy.

Emotions are important. Our emotions help us. We just need to manage them. Emotions influence a child's:

- Physical health (Olds et al., 2004; Raine et al., 2001)
- Mental health (Cole & Hall, 2008; Keenan, 2000)
- Social competence (Halberstadt et al., 2002; Denham, 1998)
- School readiness (Blair, 2002; Raver)

Emotions provide a means to:

- Appraise our situations
- Prepare to act
- Act on our own behalf
- Communicate our internal states

(Bowlby, 1973; Campos et al., 1994; Frijda, 1986; Izard, 2001)

As the child grows, so does their ability to self-regulate. In toddlerhood and in the preschool years, the child's emotional regulatory system starts to mature, and the burden of emotional regulation begins to shift from parent to child. The child is learning to manage emotions on their own. This is *not*, however, the time to abandon the child emotionally. While the child is getting better at managing emotions, they are by no means an expert. Guidance is still a requirement.

We also know a child's ability to self-regulate and calm are directly tied to language development. As children begin to develop language skills, they are better able to label their emotions, thoughts, and intentions, which helps them regulate their emotional responses. It also helps them understand the need to have and use a calming strategy. With increased language skills, children are better able to let their parents know what they need in order to calm themselves. We are talking here about the day-to-day frustrations that can sometimes send our children off the deep end. It is important to remember that children, especially children younger than five, still need their parents to help them regulate intense emotions (fear, anxiety, excitement, sadness)—the really big stuff.

It is important to note that children who have a language delay or disorder are likely to have difficulty with emotional regulation. They just don't have the language, or words, they may need to clearly communicate what they are feeling and how they may need help. In this case, it is even more important you support your children as they develop emotional regulation. You will need to help give them the language (words) they can use to describe their feelings. Developing an emotional vocabulary is key.

We can help our children learn to calm in a few ways. First, they will need a safe place to take a break when things become too much. Think back to the previous chapter when we discussed the regulation station. Your children need a place to take a break, and remember, sometimes that will be in your arms in the form of a big, deep hug. It is important to remember that even if you have a safe place, your children need to know what to do when they get there. I firmly believe you can begin to teach a calming strategy to very young children. With very young children, even months old, it begins with remaining calm yourself, picking up the dysregulated child, holding them close, and taking three very slow, deep breaths. You don't have to talk. You certainly don't have to tell the child that they are OK because the child is *not OK*. They are upset and dysregulated. So, just breathe—deeply and slowly. Then you can begin to pat the child's back and say, "Shhh, shhh, shhh," over and over. The "shhh, shhh, shhh" will mimic the mother's heartbeat, and you want the patting to be at about sixty beats per minute. You can even begin to sway, rock, or walk. The movement can be calming. This will help the child begin to understand breathing is key to calm.

SENSORY PROCESSING AND SENSORY SYSTEMS: WHAT DOES THIS MEAN?

Life has become a state of sensory overload.

—Joseph Curiale

Sensory overload can cause our nervous system
to react as if we're in danger, and it prompts us to
fight (stay and fight) or take flight (run away).

—Angela Hanscom

L ET'S TALK ABOUT OUR EIGHT sensory systems and how and what these systems are processing. I am willing to bet some of you didn't know we have eight sensory systems that work together to help us make sense of our world. And when these systems are not working correctly, we can feel overwhelmed, feel out of control, and often just shut down so we don't have to try to process incoming sensory input. Let me try to explain further.

I will start with the basics, so we are all on the same page. Sensory processing (sometimes called sensory integration, or SI) is a term that refers to the way the nervous system receives messages from the senses and turns them into appropriate motor and behavioral responses. Whether you are biting into a hamburger, riding a bicycle, or reading a book, your successful completion of the activity requires processing sensation or sensory integration. Sensory processing disorder (SPD, formerly known as sensory integration dysfunction) is a condition that exists when sensory signals *don't* get organized into appropriate responses. Pioneering occupational therapist and neuroscientist A. Jean Ayres, PhD, likened SPD to a neurological traffic jam that prevents certain parts of the brain from receiving the information needed to interpret sensory information correctly. An individual with SPD may find it difficult to process and act upon information received through the senses. This can create challenges in performing everyday tasks. If SPD is not recognized and treated, motor difficulties, behavioral problems, anxiety, depression, and school failure may result. For those with sensory processing disorder, sensory information goes into the brain but does not get organized into appropriate responses.

What does this actually look like? This is a typical sensory processing response:

- The neurological system takes in the information. Example: It is really hot outside!
- The brain organizes the information and makes sense of it. We begin to sweat.
- We respond accordingly to our environment. We find a way to cool off.

More times than not, a typically developing sensory system just works. In other words, we don't really have to think about it. If the light is too bright, we cover our eyes. If the siren is too loud, we cover our ears. We don't even have to think about the response. The senses communicate with the brain and generate an appropriate response.

As I mentioned, we have eight sensory systems. In school, most of us learned about our five senses, and we were pretty sure that is all we had. We learned about these five senses and what they did when they were working correctly and communicating with our brain to generate appropriate responses. We weren't taught the ways in which the senses actually interact with each other and how this can impact our behavior. The five senses we studied in school are very important, but we have to add the additional three sensory systems to get a complete picture. Here's a list of the eight sensory systems:

- visual (sight)
- touch (tactile)
- hearing (auditory)
- taste (gustatory)
- smell (olfactory)
- vestibular (balance)
- proprioceptive (body awareness)
- interoceptive (state of internal organs: pain, heat, illness, hunger, toileting, etc.)

For some of us, the brain has trouble organizing and responding to information that comes in from these eight sensory systems. Sometimes there are certain sounds (someone chewing, nails on a chalkboard, dripping water), sights (bright lights, flickering lights, certain colors), smells (certain foods, perfume, scented cleaning products), textures (tags in clothes, the rib in a sock, soft fabrics, silky fabrics, rough fabrics, hard and crunchy foods, soft and mushy foods), and tastes (sweet, salty, sharp-tasting foods, spicy foods, or something bitter) that can create a feeling of sensory overload. Bright or flickering lights, loud noises, certain textures of food, and scratchy clothing are just some of the triggers that can make us feel overwhelmed and upset. This is especially true with children who don't have the language (words) to tell you exactly what is bothering them.

The truth is we all have sensory stuff—all of us. For example, I am what most call a picky eater. By this, I mean I like hard and crunchy foods. If it looks like it will feel funny in my mouth, there is *no way* I am eating it. I am not eating tapioca. What is that! I don't like mushy fruit like cooked apples. I will not be eating a strawberry; it has seeds. I don't really care for hot beverages—no coffee, tea, or hot chocolate. I like ice and cold and bubbles. I know, I know. I have lived my life with people saying how crazy it is, but, you guys, it's real.

I bet you all have sensory stuff too. Some of you are bothered by people chewing loudly. Some of you don't like large crowds. Others of you are particular about the fabrics you wear. The list goes on and on. The takeaway from this is that even typically developing children have sensory preferences and will avoid other sensations they find bothersome. Be respectful and try to help them learn to tolerate certain sensory experiences without demanding they tolerate something that will cause a complete meltdown.

It is important to know there are really three general types of sensory processing challenges, and many kids experience a mix of all of them. One is oversensitivity (hypersensitivity). A child with hypersensitivity can be sensory avoiding. This means the child will avoid sensory input because it's too overwhelming. Another is undersensitivity (hyposensitivity). A child who is hyposensitive will be what we call sensory seeking. This means the child looks for more sensory stimulation. A third is underresponsive. A child who is underresponsive is often oblivious to any input and often appears lazy or tired.

Avoiding behaviors, seeking behaviors, underresponsive behaviors, and a combination of the three help to keep children regulated. When they get too much or too little sensory input, this throws them off, and they fight, take flight, or freeze. These behavioral reactions can be disruptive to both a child and to you. Understanding that the cause of some of your child's frustrations or challenges could be due to his sensory system misfiring can help you to help the child. Step back and take a closer look at how your child is reacting to a particular situation or event and see if there may be a sensory connection.

In some cases, it is not just a mild reaction to the tags in his shirts or a dislike for mushy foods. Sometimes a child has a true sensory processing disorder. This can be determined by an occupational therapist who is trained in sensory processing disorders. This is not a medical diagnosis; rather, it is a determination, and an occupational therapist can be very helpful to your child. This type of professional can create a sensory diet that will help your child regulate the sensory information and can give you some excellent strategies that will make life a bit easier for both you and your child.

It is important to note that if you suspect your child is having difficulty with more than the tags in their shirts and mushy food, you may want to find a great occupational therapist and have your child evaluated. Understand sensory processing disorder comes with difficulties that can put your child at a higher risk for many emotional, social, and educational problems, including the inability to make friends or be a part of a group, poor self-concept, academic failure, and being labeled clumsy, uncooperative, belligerent, disruptive, or out of control. Anxiety, depression, aggression, or other behavioral problems can follow. Parents may be blamed for their child's behavior by people who are unaware of the child's hidden handicap.

While we all have sensory stuff, children with SPD need additional support. It is also important to note many children on the autism spectrum also have SPD. However, not all children with SPD are on the autism spectrum.

Here are some basic examples:

Tactile (Touch)

Avoider Hypersensitive	Seeker Hyposensitive	Underresponsive
• Avoids touch • Doesn't like to be dirty • Doesn't like tags in clothes • Doesn't like to be barefoot • Avoids sand tables, water play, and sensory tubs • Is a picky eater	• Puts objects in mouth • Bumps into people or objects • Seeks out textures with a strong feedback • Is a close-talker • Rubs or bite their own skin (likes the way it feels) • Needs to touch *everything*	• Slow to potty train (doesn't feel the need to go) • Unaware of the difference in textures • Unaware of being messy • Poor fine motor skills (can't feel the pencil) • No response to gentle touch

Auditory (Hearing)

Avoider Hypersensitive	Seeker Hyposensitive	Underresponsive
• Whispers (speaking loudly vibrates in the ears) • Covers ears or needs headphones frequently • Cries when they hear loud noises	• Likes being in noisy places or crowds • Speaks loudly (has difficulty with inside voice) • Prefers television or music to be loud	• Tunes in to unusual sounds or rhythms • Unaware of typical sounds in the room or outside • Responds slowly or not at all to verbal requests

Visual (Sight)

Avoider Hypersensitive	Seeker Hyposensitive	Underresponsive
• Avoids eye contact • Avoids bright lights • Covers eyes • Unable to determine distance • May get nauseous or a headache from overuse of eyes	• Stares at bright lights or flickering lights • Looks at things close-up • Watches objects as they move through lights	• Can appear to be staring off in space • Slow response to or difficulty getting out of the way of moving objects • Unaware of new objects

Vestibular (Movement and Balance)

Avoider Hypersensitive	Seeker Hyposensitive	Underresponsive
• Appears slow or lazy • Fearful of elevators or escalators • Becomes car sick easily • Has poor balance • Fearful of movement or of falling	• Enjoys being dizzy • In constant motion • Rocks • Spins • Is hyperactive • Takes movement activities to the extreme • Is a risk-taker	• Accident-prone • Can appear lazy and tired • Less coordinated • Dislikes new movement experiences

Proprioceptive (Body Position)

Avoider Hypersensitive	Seeker Hyposensitive	Underresponsive
• Prefers not to move • Dislikes others helping to move them • Is a picky eater • Appears lazy and overtired	• Engages in extreme rough-and-tumble play • Likes to crash into things or people • Uses aggressive behaviors • Wants to be hugged hard or wrapped tightly • Bites nails and/or fingers • Chews on objects	• Has little to no response to significant injury • Is not aware of being touched • Has difficulty with gross motor skills • Has poor fine motor skills

Remember, a child can be an avoider in one area and a seeker in another area. A few of the areas overlap and work together.

The takeaway from this chapter is a simple one. We all have our own unique sensory stuff that makes us who we are. Your child is no different. If you don't like the feel of wet grass on your bare feet and your level of anxiety shoots through the roof thinking about the possibility of even having to walk outside with bare feet, know your child has the same reaction to their own sensory stuff. The real difference is the child doesn't have the coping skills, the language, or the strategies to avoid that which can cause them stress or anxiety. Be respectful of these differences. Help your child learn to tolerate things that are unpleasant, but don't expect your child will just get over it. You haven't.

THE END IS JUST THE BEGINNING

Every new beginning comes from
some other beginning's end.

—Seneca

Each morning we are born again. What
we do today is what matters most.

—Buddha

THE GIFT OF PARENTING

WE MADE IT TO THE end, which for many of you is the beginning. Maybe it is the end of doing things the way you have been doing them and the beginning of trying new things, looking at things in a different way, or affirming you knew it all along. This book has been a labor of love for me. It took me way too long to write, but I have come to the conclusion that I needed the time. I needed the time to decide what I thought was most important to share. I needed the time to decide if I wanted to give a voice to what I know to be true and necessary. I needed time to be sure I wanted people to know just how important our littlest people are. I needed time to carefully choose the topics to focus on. I just needed the time.

Since I started this book, both of my beautiful daughters have married, and my older daughter has had two beautiful daughters of her own. I am now a grandparent (a.k.a. Lolly), and words can't express just how blessed I feel to have the opportunity to (grand)parent again. I have learned so much since my first opportunity to parent and am eager to share what I have learned.

I have always had a heart for the littles. They are such a sweet blessing and are also so challenging. They live in the moment and keep us focused on what really matters. Just think about how much they learn in five short years. They go from being totally and completely dependent on us to learning to walk, talk, sing, dance, manage their emotions, and push our buttons. So many first times happen in the first five years, and it is such a wonderful blessing to be able to share these experiences with our children. Don't get so lost in the challenges that you miss the joys and frustrations of these early years. It is a time of such tremendous growth for both you and your child. Give yourself a break, take a deep breath, and try again. Give your child a break, help them take a deep breath, and try again.

You're in this together, and parenting is no joke. Your goal is to raise a good human. You decide what that looks like and keep your eye on the prize.

Our children give us the opportunity to become
the parents we always wished we'd had.

—Louise Hart

If you had amazing parents, lucky you. You have great models, and your children will be truly blessed. If you were not blessed with parents who cherished you, here is your opportunity to improve on the generation. Be the parent you wished you had. You know what that looks like, so don't lose sight of it. Your child is depending on you. Be well. Be blessed. Be grateful.

REFERENCES

Bailey, Becky. A. 2001. *Conscious Discipline: 7 Basic Skills for Brain Smart Classroom Management.* Oviedo, FL: Loving Guidance.

Bandura, Albert. 1977. *Social Learning Theory.* Englewood Cliffs, NJ: Prentice Hall.

Basu, Tanya. 2019. "Screen time might be physically changing kids' brains." *Technology Review.* www.technologyreview.com.

Carey, Bjorn. 2013. "Language Gap between Rich and Poor Children Begins in Infancy, Stanford Psychologists Find." *Stanford News,* September 25, 2013.

Center on the Developing Child, Harvard University. 2020. "Resilience." developingchild.harvard.edu/science/key-concepts/resilience/.

Crain, William. 1992. *Theories of Development: Concepts and Applications.* 3rd ed. Englewood Cliffs, NJ: Prentice Hall.

Duckworth, Angela. 2016. *Grit: The Power of Passion and Perseverance.* New York: Scribner.

Guerra, Jennifer. 2012. "Five Things to Know about Early Childhood Brain Development." State of Opportunity, November 14, 2012.

Hurley, Katie. 2015. *The Happy Kid Handbook: How to Raise Joyful Children in a Stressful World.* New York: Penguin Publishing Group.

Hurley, Katie. 2020. "Resilience in Children: Strategies to Strengthen Your Kids." Psycom, November 24, 2020. www.psycom.net/build-resilience-children.

Hutton, John, Johnathan Dudley, and Tzipi Horowitz-Kraus. 2019. "Associations between screen-based media use and brain white matter integrity in preschool-aged children." *JAMA Pediatrics* 174, no. 5 (May 1, 2020): 509.

LaMotte, Sandee. 2019. "MRIs Show Screen Time Linked to Lower Brain Development in Preschoolers." CNN, November 4, 2019.

National Institutes of Health. 2020. "Brain Basics: Know Your Brain." NIH.gov, February 13, 2020.

Seligman, Martin. 1991. *Learned Optimism: How to Change Your Mind and Your Life*. New York: Penguin Random House.

Shonkoff, Jack. 2009. "Investment in Early Childhood Development Lays the Foundation for a Prosperous and Sustainable Society." *Encyclopedia on Early Childhood Development*.

Tarbox, Jonathan. 2009. "Comparing Indirect, Descriptive, and Experimental Functional Assessments of Challenging Behavior in Children with Autism." *Journal of Developmental and Physical Disabilities* 21, no. 6: 493–514.

Wilmot, Keri, ed. 2020. "Understanding Sensory Processing Issues." Understood. www.understood.org/en/learning-thinking-differences/child-learning-disabilities/sensory-processing-issues/understanding-sensory-processing-issues.

Young, Karen. 2018. https://www.heysigmund.com/the-proven-way-to-build-resilience.

Young, Sarah. 2020. "Screen time among toddlers has more than doubled since 1997." Consumer Affairs. www.consumeraffairs.com

Printed in the United States
by Baker & Taylor Publisher Services